TALK
YOUR WAY
TO SUCCESS
WITH PEOPLE

Talk
Your Way To
Success With People

J. V. Cerney

Parker Publishing Company, Inc., West Nyack, N.Y.

PRINTED IN THE UNITED STATES OF AMERICA

B & P

To my daughter, Pat.

Other Books By The Author:

*How to Develop a Million Dollar
   Personality*

*Confidence and Power for
   Successful Living*

*Dynamic Laws of
   Thinking Rich*

*Stay Young . . . Live Longer
   Through Mental Self-Conditioning*

*Care and Prevention of
   Athletic Injuries*

What This Book
Will Do For
Your Freeway To Fame

Here's the route

In your hands at this moment is a freeway to personal power: a pulsing, vivacious action toward the popularity you desire—a miracle of achieving, living, loving, and finding happiness—a throughway to destiny and the goals you would reach.

How? Words! Yes, I said WORDS . . . W-O-R-D-S . . . those giants of communication—the beginning and end of social intercourse—words ranging from gentle endearment to cataclysmic explosions that can rock the world with the dynamite of a new kind of living—virile words giving birth to achievement—words that are the seeds of the kind of living you want—words that accomplish—words that create and procreate—psychological explosives that can take you to fame and fortune or abort you into mediocrity—words designed not just to dazzle destiny but to achieve the simplest wants. WORDS! Your route to the future.

1. *This Book* will plant new ideas, new concepts, a new belief and feeling of security which you need to succeed. It will develop your Personality Appeal.

2. *This Book* will stimulate your enthusiasm and make your self-belief grow strong. You will power up with self-confidence to become a winner and make that Impression Circle around you glow.

3. *This Book* will open up new avenues of thinking and

give you a roadway to follow. It will explain the compelling urgencies that make you want the better things in life. Your life will be on fire with gutsy concepts for tomorrow.

4. *This Book* will help you overcome the hazards of living in a goldfish bowl as you climb the pyramid. It will supply know-how that turns your talents into productive results as its powerful principles point the way to tomorrow.

Anyone can use these techniques and be a winner!

Step into your new life now with full confidence that you CAN have success, that you will be able to recognize opportunity and use it to your advantage, that you already have the strength and capacity to win. Every principle in this book helps you do just this. Every principle is yours to be used—so use them! Use this book in social, business, professional or industrial power moves, whether you are a rich man, a poor man, a beggar or a thief. Develop the principles in this book. Let them spell out a glorious new life. Be warned in advance that as you take advantage of this plan-of-action you will find surging new strengths developing within yourself, strengths you didn't think were possible, so don't be afraid of them. Harness these strengths. Plan and organize your life around them and put these enormous new-found capacities to work!

This book is extraordinary

You will find that *this book is NOT ordinary*. In its plan-of-action it brings you lusty ideas to help you organize your thinking and your life. Some of the ideas are new. Some are old. All of them are tried and true to give you a dramatic and dynamic way to use words as the foundation for a whole new life, a vibrant, fruitful life, where your Golden Goals come true and your wants are all achieved. *This is not a book of vocabulary!* It is NOT a book of grammar! Instead it's a book of what you can do with words to make them pay off in talking your way to success with people.

Exactly what DO you want out of life? Do you want recognition, self-confidence, personal power, a million-dollar personality? Do you want to dump your old way of life and move up front where the action is? Well you can have all this and heaven too, but remember that yesterday's world will change radically as you set your new plan-of-action into motion. You will be fired up for the miracle of better living. You will not just think big. You will BE big in the doing. You will be on your way to success because you stop to learn how to talk to people.

So on your mark . . .
Get set . . ·

Go into action now with an open mind. Put the following ideas to work. MAKE them work! With each new achievement feel your self-confidence and assurance grow. Feel your personal power develop. Like a life-giving transfusion, experience the flow of strength that the magic power of words can give you. Dazzle destiny by moving into a whole new life . . . a whole new world . . . the sparkling new world of words that awaits you!

Contents

    PEAL" AND HOW YOUR "IMPRESSION CIRCLE"
    WORKS (*Continued*)

    *cations. What are the properties of personality appeal?
    Why learn the art of communication in personality
    appeal? Your voice . . . passport to success. Your voice
    is a persuasive power . . . use it! How does your voice
    actually affect people? Loyalty is born and conceived
    in words.*

4. THERE'S NO BUSINESS LIKE "SNOW" BUSINESS   33

    *Gutsy press agentry pays! The lone ranger rides again!
    Can your "snow jobs" be booby-trapped? Develop your
    plan-of-action long in advance. Pathway to power
    through speech. How to use descriptive language. Per-
    suasiveness with people is an acquired characteristic.
    Design your personality pitch to earn bigger payoffs.
    Use words to get at people's emotions. The meek will
    never inherit the earth. You are the key in career con-
    trol. Language is volatile expression. So why not USE
    WORDS?*

5. DEVELOPING THE ORAL FORMULA FOR
    SUCCESS   49

    *The silent senses play a coy role in the trek to success.
    How do you know the goal you have chosen is right?
    Then what's the answer? Self-concepts emerge from
    self-understanding. As far as you are concerned, you
    are the center of the world! Force now takes on a
    new character. Is there such a formula? Five words
    that master your destiny. Just exactly what happens
    through words? How do your words influence people?
    The "Persuaders" and how they operate. The "Inform-
    ers" and how they can be used. The "Excitement-
    maintainers" and their purpose. The "Responders" or*

Develop enthusiasm in daily living. Establish contact through devices at your command. The social color of words and how they brighten your life to lower your tensions. What is color in words? Harness color and you harness power. How tranquilizer pills effectively kill words and the success-drive. Are pills the passport to tension release? Tranquilizers are a hindrance to progress. You have to face up to facts to survive. How to be sharp about flat emotional notes. You are never alone.

Press the buttons of the trigger zones. Stand up now and be counted. Your voice and its contribution to persuasion. Intimate tricks in the vocal department. How to approach your audience. Use the words they know. How to activate people through words.

Technique for speech-making. How to punch across a point. Motivate your audience. What is it that people want most? Speak up! Make every word count. Turn your own lights on to light the world. Move in on your audience with strong vocal action. Put your quarry on target when you fire. The vocal approach to being more compelling. How do you characterize yourself as a speaker? Remember! Your voice is NOT what it sounds like to YOU! Your voice must carry the mark of distinction. Words are wants. Most word-forces are controllable.

TALK
YOUR WAY
TO SUCCESS
WITH PEOPLE

1

The Magic
Power of Words

The greatest power at man's disposal is neither electricity, water, atomic energy or the mighty resources of the earth. It's *WORDS!* . . . word-power as the vehicle to success! . . . a power without peer as man reaches eagerly over his daily horizons into the unending magic of tomorrow . . . *POWER, THAT LASTS A LIFETIME* in his efforts to be a winner.

W ords, man's invention, are his medium of exchange. They are his life and everything making up his life: words of wisdom—words of sincerity, courtesy, respect and appreciation—words of humor, hate and thanks—words by which to be born and words by which to die—words to destroy—words that are dynamic, resplendent, glad—words that are soft, persuasive, gentle and kind—religious words—delicate words—mighty words—gaunt words—words of heaven and hell, glory and defeat—words that are cruel, crude, dull, disgusting, repulsive and harsh—words of science—words of love—all of them vibrant, all of them pregnant with meaning, all of them different, each word passing on into tomorrow without a duplicate and yet with very little change.

No one changes the force of words but they *can* be controlled, and in the velvet-lined prison of life words are the greatest power the world has ever known. As long as man lives, so do they. As long as he exists they go on . . . and then some.

Because of this you have to remember that wherever people go, go words. Where words go, goes persuasion and influence and the genesis of change and that which is new. Words are power, and the source of power, and there is no end to their energy.

As you become more and more aware of this, and aware of their source within you, and their relationship to that which is around you, you will begin to realize how you are intimately tied to words and that *through words you manipulate the means to meet the ends you desire*. Through words comes the understanding that you have only to use their magic for personal benefit, and it's at this point that our story begins.

From this moment on
be aware that:

In using words to achieve success you have only to know yourself and understand the giant that is within you. Why?

Words are:

POWER *usable on people to guarantee YOUR future*
. . . as well as theirs

POWER *that YOU can harness and control*

POWER *convertible into your Golden Goals as you coordinate time, place, and occasion*

POWER *you can switch on and off at will as you move toward the future . . . incredible strength just waiting for you to release it.*

POWER *superseded by nothing ever known, an irreducible, unlimited, fantastic giant providing a magic key to success.*

You don't believe it? Then here's evidence:

William James once said that we are only half awake. He was kind. Actually the average man is less then half awake. He releases only a third of his potential. His subconscious urges, his talents, his abilities to use words to get him what he wants lie latent and dormant. Once awakened, the words he generates can become volatile, explosive, active. They become stimuli to the opportunities of tomorrow. They become his power.

Realizing that you are only half awake means you have a vast potential waiting to be used. How well you take advantage of this potential determines your success! How well you weave the magic of words as the powerful influence on all this determines fortune and fame. It's a strange and compelling magic, this magic of self-control, and all it takes is coming awake. All it takes is the realization, and then the use, of the powers within you.

**Do you know YOUR
latent powers?**

Do you know yourself? Do you know the words that can help you? Are you ready to harness the dynamo of your mind to your personality and turn on enthusiasm, courage and charm? Are you ready to climb the social, professional or business pyramid to a defined goal? Are you ready to lead? Can you manipulate people? Have you awakened more then one-third of your potential to guarantee your fortune and fame?

If you haven't, then let's probe the depths of your influence a bit more: Is your power of persuasion sufficient to help people form an opinion about you? Are you well enough informed so that you are able to put an idea across that people can grasp? Do you give others the feeling of trustworthiness through what you do and say? Do they feel your strength and the power of your persuasion? Do they sense the excellence of your judgment as you put ideas into words they understand? Does what you have to say make sense? Is your message worthwhile? Are you getting through?

If your answers have been all essentially positive, then you have begun to develop your latent powers. You have begun to develop your potential. You have begun to develop your capabilities and are just now beginning to feel that amazing power that awaits within you. More than this, it indicates you are on your way to success.

If some of your answers have been negative, then this is *your* book! What you can do to change those negatives to positives are found in the following text. What you can do to develop a dynamic new life is mapped out for you step by step. From this moment on you will be wrapped up in the practical psychology of words.

You will become more vivacious, more capable of communicating. You will develop a personality breakthrough and use your voice as a passport to success! You will learn to create an indelible impression, to be persuasive, to sell yourself through the explosive dramatics of words! You will develop your own hotline to people and learn how to deliver a "snow job"! You will learn the FIVE MAGIC WORDS IN THE FORMULA FOR SUCCESS and develop a million-dollar personality out of "snow"! You will begin to think big and develop power concepts. You will develop three strategic moves for getting through to people and formulate a gold-plated approach to being a "wanted man"! You will learn from this book how to recognize the hidden persuaders and then put them to work. You will learn about the great motivators and how you can turn them to your advantage. Take this book now and learn about *words*. Learn that words are the paintbrush of social intercourse. Use words as the bridge to people. Break the sound barriers and pull heart strings. Persuade! It's all waiting for you, so move on! . . . Success is waiting!

The Psychology Of Words
Is Persuasive

Words are mental manipulators. Professor John Tyndale, the English scientist, used to tell about the psychology of words used by his servant. Each morning the elderly man would knock on the professor's door and say: "Arise, sir. It is near seven o'clock. You have great work to do this day!"

You too have great work to do this day. You too have to learn to use words to tell your story. You have to learn to paint with words, to portray, to deliver a message.

When Tzu Chang asked Confucius the meaning of the word *virtue* the sage said: "Five things constitute virtue. They are courtesy, magnanimity, sincerity, earnestness, and kindness. With courtesy you avoid insult. With magnanimity you win all. With sincerity men will come to trust you. With earnestness and kindness you can achieve success."

Note those five words: *courtesy, magnanimity, sincerity, earnestness,* and *kindness,* all of them a workshop to get what you want through words, all of them a way to "get through to people," all of them capable of being demonstrated through *words.*

A word may be praise. It may even be a cry out for help such as occurred on that cold, rainy day in 1953 when Edmund Hillary and his guide, Tensing Norgay, successfully scaled Mount Everest. They were descending when Hillary slipped. He called to his guide. The Sherpa tribesman sunk his pick in the ice. The rope held. Hillary's fall was broken. He not only owed his life to his Nepalese guide, but he owed it to calling out for help with words.

Words are constantly informative. They not only tell you that housewives use 30 million cans of food daily but that by 1975 airships will carry 200 passengers at 1,200 miles per hour. They tell you that prepackaged food will in the future come with its own heating element, that ultrasonic sound waves will replace mechanical agitation for washing clothes. All of this in words, a non-stop flow, an inexhaustible well of words that is the lifeblood of human communication. They are the pulse of social flow. Through words you live and learn. Through words you live and love. Through them you build a brave new life and stay young, and live longer, as long as you use the perpetually strong psychology of words.

"In the beginning was the word"

The big move today, in using words, is to inundate people with *information*. We are swamped with it. Newspapers, magazines, books, radio, television, each supplies it without end. "Facts" are everywhere. So is the lack of understanding of these "facts" when they are not made plain.

Confusion exists as politicians, propagandists, editors, advertisers, charity-appealers, broadcasters, and so forth, create high- and low-level monsters of *information*. These intangible monsters frighten people. Confusion results. Insecurity begins, and if you, in your particular area, would be a success you have to learn the magic power of these words and make them count. What you have to say or write has to have impact. It has to be understood so that you "get through." From beginning to end it's *the word* and YOU have to learn how to use it!

When I was a boy in Michigan, there was a grizzled old character called Trader "Spike" Horn who spoke with great authority. He was a simple, long-haired, long-bearded naturalist who hated crowds and his favorite statement about urban areas was, "Cities stink!"

One day I asked him why he had broken his vaudeville contract and returned home to Michigan. He surveyed me sharply through the overhanging filter of his eyebrows and pulled down another bear pelt for my inspection.

"I came back here to Nature," he said, "where the words and the life are simple. The Scriptures say, 'Be ye doers of the word . . .' and that's what I'm a doing. Maybe you don't remember your Scriptures too good, son. Maybe I don't neither. One thing I do remember, is—'In the beginning was the word and the word was God.' And when you get down to it, how a man acts are the words he believes. It depends on being a doer of the word. What this country needs is less lying, less cheating, more understanding, less facts and more doing. That's the word, boy. Now you wunna buy this bearskin or don't you?"

Words, the power thrust that influences people

Words are indeed the beginning and end of everything. They are powers manufactured to influence people: the mother soothing her injured child, the politician making promises in his attempt to whip up votes, public relations men doing a "snow job" to create a better image for someone or something, great writers creating books, preachers exhorting their flocks, great statesmen calling out to their people in an influential thrust of power. All of them dealing in persuasion. All of them touching on human needs. All of them with aims and goals in view.

The politician attempts to build up loyalties, trust, love, and even fear, and he does this through words.

According to Lane and Sears:* "The politician manipulates distortion, relying on the assimilation effect and minimizing the contrast effect among his public. He manipulates incredulity, using it as a cover for his varied and conflicting appeals to opposing groups. He attacks the resistance to his opinions indirectly. He seeks out those whose ties with hostile groups have already been weakened and directs his appeal to them. He makes his catchwords, his slogans, the vehicles of social communication. He provides formulae for easing specific reference group conflicts. He suggests other targets for the hostile, reassures the insecure, invites the lonely into the party, tells everyone that he loves them." And this, essentially, is what you are doing, too.

In this way the politician leaves an impression on the public mind. He does it by anchoring a word to its voting finger at election time. That word is his name, his ideas, the image, his personality. It's the circle of impression he creates. It's the use he makes of the magic of words that captivate and conquer. But it's not just politicians who use *the Word!* It's also YOU! YOU have to captivate and conquer people! You have to learn to use the fantastic power of words as a vehicle in moving up to the success you desire! YOU have to use your head as you use the magic power of words because on the tip of your tongue, the form of your lips, and the air and voice box that makes it all possible is enough power to last a lifetime!

---

* Robert Lane and David O. Sears, *Public Opinion* (Englewood Cliffs, N.J.: Prentice-Hall, Inc., 1964), p. 56.

2

Captivate And Conquer With A Package Of P/R

There is nothing man does in which words do not directly or indirectly play a role. By themselves words are useless. Like sleeping dynamos they lie quiescent and ready for use. Once awakened, their potential for generating energy springs eternally alive. To captivate and conquer you have to develop a public relations package that will achieve success.

9

M orris says, "Words intervene in almost everything that has to do with human behavior."* He believes that words unto themselves are unique. Yet to define a word it is necessary to use more words to explain it. In explaining a word you find yourself developing a new awareness of words as well as a growing comprehension about yourself and other people. You begin to realize what words are and how they play a vital role in your life. Even more than this you become aware of the need to use words on other people and how words are placed in a personal package of public relations if you would make it big in the future.

Through words personalities become more vivacious, sunsets more brilliant when described, a woman more lovely when her charms are pointed out, an experience more intimate when portrayed in the living color of vocal expression. Oral sounds create a descriptive flow. They create a conditioning force, a highly sensitive and expressive medium designed to net specific ends.

You've heard it said that silence is golden? For whom? How long? Create a vacuum of sound and what do you have? Live as a hermit and you exist. You do not live. Take words away and you are a vegetable!

As long as you can use words, or even abuse them, you are animate. You are still moving into the future, still articulate. When you can no longer use words to stimulate thinking and the imagination you are over the hill. Your public relations program is dead and so are you, so let's start from there. From this moment on let's stop being a vegetable among the living dead. Let's captivate and conquer people through the personalized guided missiles of sound. Let's use words to advantage!

Words are intimate and personal

As personal tools words are instruments of communication with which to reach out and touch those you would motivate to action,

---

* Charles Morris, *The Open Shelf* (Englewood Cliffs, N.J.: Prentice-Hall, Inc., 1948), p. 54.

those whom you would love, those whom you would persuade to do something beneficial for you as well as for them. When there is a lack of words, a paucity, the person possessed of such a lack becomes less and less capable of success in a more and more complex world. Because of this the blind have to learn Braille. The deaf get hearing aids and *learn* to say words with their hands. Children go to school for the vocabulary that will become their social, religious, professional, business and industrial links with the future. Scientists use terminology that describes their work.

All life must have expression. Without words, or their facsimiles, there is no communication. You personally cannot understand others. Most of all you can't understand yourself and you will not believe this until you see words in action. You will not comprehend the vast power and influence of words, and their meanings and interpretations until you put them to work. Such words rule your life and create consequences: words that flowed from the mouths and pens of people like Socrates, Demosthenes, Voltaire, Schopenhauer, Douglass, Roosevelt, Sinclair Lewis, Hemingway, and Steinbeck. You will not be totally conscious of their power until you witness them generate opportunity or contribute to failure as happened in the catastrophe of Germany and the obliteration of millions of Jews under Hitler's rule.

You will not be sure until you see how words make personal power materialize from desire, how they stimulate urgencies and drives, how they are persuasive, how they are controls over situations controllable by words, how they are used to achieve wants—YOUR WANTS—whether your want is for gold, for understanding, for love, trust or just for fun. You will not believe this until you put your own personal public relations program, your P/R, to work.

Professor Kelly Jamison punches this across when he says: "The moment you develop this awareness of words your personal drive for achievement begins. When this happens you're on your way to talking yourself up to success. That's the moment your timid probes into the future become more authoritative, when they become personal forces, convincing, forceful strengths in which you command attention. At this point is the beginning of your consciousness of personal power. Words are this power. They are controls. As encapsulated energy they await being triggered into a train of events designed to aid your future. When this happens you are no longer a vegetable. You life has begun! Through words you become capable of controlling almost everything and this also includes emotion."

How can you determine emotional health through words?

Making a self-inventory is often an inadequate gymnastic approach to understanding yourself but there IS a way of achieving this self-awareness through words as you develop your P/R package. This self-awareness can come through questions used to determine whether your career-health is up to par, whether success will be easier to attain, whether you are subject to change.

Let's take a group of words now and call it a "chart." This chart is composed of questions that have no particular purpose at this moment other than to tickle your emotional "trigger zones." Answer the questions rapidly. DO NOT PAUSE. Go through them without debate as you make this initial experiment.

SELF-AWARENESS CHART

FOR EMOTIONAL STABILITY

	YES	NO
1. I have difficulty being friendly with people	____	____
2. I have very few real friends	____	____
3. Very few people like me	____	____
4. At night I dream the craziest dreams	____	____
5. Sometimes I have visions	____	____
6. People don't understand me at all	____	____
7. Some say I'm peculiar	____	____
8. I know people are laughing at me	____	____
9. A lot of the time when I'm with people I feel sick or weak	____	____
10. I just can't seem to get up and talk to people in public	____	____
11. I blush easily	____	____
12. Sometimes I walk in my sleep	____	____

13. Sometimes I think my parents aren't mine   ____ ____
14. I keep wanting to run away from it all   ____ ____

> NOTE: *If you have marked any of the above positively you would appear to be emotionally unstable. Your answers would tend to indicate that your possibilities for success are not so strong as they should be, that emotional strain is strong within you, and that you have to readjust. But let's prove this is wrong! Let's see what develops as you put your personal P/R package to work! Let's see what this book can do for you!*

With this tentative self-awareness in mind now let's move forward. Step by step, chapter by chapter, let's prove that as you use more and more words, and learn to understand yourself and understand people, that when you finish this book you can come back to this questionnaire and not answer it the same way at all!

Let's start now! Make your new life come alive! Let's live for tomorrow! Let's create tomorrow! Let's make tomorrow vibrant with the end-products of words as you talk yourself up to success and that which you want most.

Success is a constant tour of duty

The rewards are wonderful when achievement pays off. It's simply great to be alive and be a success and if you would continue to have achievements and their rewards, you have to keep them constant. Your success drive has to be kept steady because success is a continuous route. It's an unceasing tour of duty.

No one can afford to be so self-entranced, or so confined in self-awareness, that he forgets to move up to the next goal. Lying on the oars as an excuse for resting may very well lose a race.

You've heard it said that nothing succeeds like success? This is true. It's also true that *nothing fades as fast as success when there is not a constant schedule of achievement* and any Hollywood star will attest to this dictum. Stop being seen publicly, stop advertising your product and you're soon forgotten.

The point is—if you get recognition, say thanks for the plaudits and the profits and move on. Advertising executive Charley Hunsecker says: "If you earn some measure of recognition for performance, get enjoyment out of what you have created and what you are doing. Then make your next performance that little bit better. Talk yourself up to raising your standards. Give it the right words and the right music to make accomplishment bigger and better than before."

No matter how tremendous your accomplishment is, it is only accomplishment up to the date it occurs!

Success is only what has happened so far and tomorrow is another day! So avoid the kick in the pants that comes with resting on your laurels and "letting down." Avoid being so self-entranced that a kick in the pants is necessary. Success is a constant road, so move out for new horizons! The future is where you live and it comes on one day at a time. Use each day and the words and the music that go with it to talk yourself up to success with people. Use the power of words in your personal P/R package to reach your Golden Goals.

A middle-aged enterpriser we'll call Harry Jacobsen saw an advertisement in the Wall Street Journal. It was for a franchise restaurant catering to businessmen. The menu was simple—steak, baked potato and a salad . . . $1.39. The franchise cost Harry ten grand and the turnkey operation clicked from the day it opened. Resplendent in the trappings of the gay nineties, "Gentleman Jim's" started off with a door-buster business. It was Diamond Jim Brady all over again, with Jacobsen carrying it a step further. He delivered his own personal public relations package. He dressed in top hat and tails and greeted his guests at the door with, "Hello, Senator!" Jacobsen was indeed a promoter.

Every male patron was a senator and that personalized attention turned "Gentleman Jim's" into a gold mine. Jacobsen opened units in other towns. He compounded success by developing a chain within a chain. He reached his Golden Goals by moving constantly into the future.

**Never permit negative
emotions to show**

Every business, every profession and every social situation presents problems. Jacobsen's was no exception. He had to cope with raw situations that taxed his patience and his hello-senator-charm. He could not afford to let negative emotions show, and this is a prerequisite in your personal P/R package.

Social equilibrium is often lost at the wrong time and whether it is a gorgeous lady saying "No!" to your proposition or a major advertiser flatly turning you down, the problem's the same. The way to handle it is also the same.

Simply mask your emotions. Don't retreat. Launch an offensive and take the other person by surprise. Use words to shift the pattern of thinking. Use words to make the other person more aware of you. Here's how one public relations specialist of an advertising agency handled his client. In breezy Jimmy Clancy's own words:

"My ulcer was burning rocket fuel in my belly but I maintained my cool and gave the client my love-and-kisses routine. This busts him wide open. There he was expecting me to blow my top because he said no to our agency package. He knew it cost a bundle to develop. But I didn't blow my top and this shakes him up. He starts the appeasement policy and this gets my foot back in the door. I simply traded on *his* emotions. With words I went to work. With my ace-in-the-hole reserved for this moment I moved in and turned it on. I said to him:

"Of course, what our agency man just showed you isn't *your* kind of package, Mr. Big! Not *your* kind of advertising at all! You need the personalized touch, the human angle. You need to get where people live, right? You want to get to their purses by way of their needs . . . even if we have to create the need. Right?

"All right, Mr. Big; here's the ticket. We're going to make your advertising dollar pay off."

Jimmy went on to explain his pitch.

"So I gave him both barrels. It's all words, see? The big sell— the power move—the verbal persuaders that turn a possible loss into profitable gain, oral morsels that promise enchanted earnings and high volume sales. I wrapped him up in the idea. I engulfed him with my moxie about his market and public wants. I let him know we had to capitalize on these wants. I demonstrated the points one by one until his resistance simply wore away. I made comparisons. I developed contrasts. I kept him off balance until he finally said, 'It looks good to me,' and that's when the boys from the agency moved in. Me? I'm strictly public relations. I wiggle the truth around until it looks good."

Some may call this "high pressure" but it isn't. The word technique that Jimmy Clancy used was strictly his kind of personal public relations package with the intensity dial turned to "full."

High-pressure salesmanship is when a person or organization uses words to lay down policy and rules AGAINST someone else's desire or way of thinking. It's force-tactics. It's an assault. It's an obnoxious and disagreeable affront to intelligence, but Jimmy played it differently.

What I'm referring to is Clancy's "wiggling the truth around until it looks good." I'm talking about the public relations man's use of words, the injection of images while the receiver's mind remains comfortably open and unopposed. Mr. Big was at ease and receptive to Clancy's ideas.

When *you* use words you can develop a personal public relations package that can take you to the moon. You can develop personal power by talking your way to success with people. You can captivate and conquer.

Developing Your Personal Public Relations Package

What is public relations and what does it have to do with personal success? Plenty!

"Public relations is a phenomenon and a necessity of our times," according to authority Philip Lesly,* and you can no longer do without it if you would be a front-line runner as a union boss, an account executive, a discount house operator, P.T.A. leader, or preacher of the gospel.

We live in a different kind of day than did the Horatio Algers (Ford, Fricke, Rockefeller, Hannah, Astor, etc.) of yesterday. It's a day of we-the-people rather than of cabbages and kings and industrial tycoons. It's a day of manipulative forces in which everybody is telling somebody something.

Once upon a time the public relations game was strictly publicity. A few newspapers were hit for space and press clips were

---

* Philip Lesly, *Public Relations Handbook* (Englewood Cliffs, N.J.: Prentice-Hall, Inc., 1962), p. 5.

your proud possessions. That's changed now. The P/R story, if it is to be told, has become more complex. Now the desire of industry or individuals using public relations procedures is to *inspire goodwill, develop beneficial images, show a more benevolent community face, develop attitude, opinions and desires, stimulate new wants, educate and guide if possible.*

Along with a thousand other duties this is part of the commercial P/R package. For the individual in his relationship to society, to his profession, business or industry, the story is the same.

As science gives us greater control over matter, machines and methods, according to Lesly, *we must learn with increasing effectiveness to control people* and this is exactly what we are after through the magic of words. This is what we are after in talking our way to success with people.

In developing your self-awareness to the necessities for achieving success you have to develop the public relations package that will sell on the social and business market. You have to develop your impression circle and the package of personality that controls people around you.

In selling yourself and your personality to people you have to be completely receptive to this theme, this doctrine, or you're dead. You can't make it to success otherwise.

In developing a P/R program, you, like big business, have to develop "goodwill." In others you have to develop a good opinion of you. Without this "build-up" people will buy neither you nor your product because they know nothing about you. Therefore *the image has to be created by YOU!* You have to create goodwill!

When goodwill is lost in industry there are strikes. There is labor turnover, poor morale, lowered production and property damage. When your personal goodwill is shot down, you also go down. When there's a break in the line of communication between man and wife, or between father and children the family breaks up. Trouble starts. When conflict develops, peace on earth and goodwill toward men are gone.

How do you handle loss of goodwill?

Whether you are a lone wolf or operate an industry with many people, you have to analyze this matter of communication and public relations with complete frankness. You have to ask yourself some very bold questions when you're trying to determine why you have lost someone's goodwill.

PERSONAL QUESTIONS TO HELP DETERMINE
WHY YOU HAVE LOST SOMEONE'S GOODWILL

1. *What do people REALLY think about me? What is their attitude?*
2. *Do they hold me in an unfavorable light?*
3. *Do they have a poor opinion of me or no opinion at all?*
4. *How and why did this come about?*
5. *Can I modify or change the situation to erase misunderstanding or misinterpretation?*
6. *How can I build a million-dollar public relations package to create the image I want?*
7. *Do I realize that with a little planning, a little guidance, less false pride, and the proper use of words to talk my way to success, that I can click in big time?*

For a comprehensive beginning in handling yourself and your own P/R package, here's where to start:

Your first step:

THE I'S HAVE IT IN
DEFINING PERSONAL OBJECTIVES

Honestly admit to yourself:

- *I want recognition!*
- *I want prestige and the good image!*
- *I want the goodwill of people!*
- *I want to prevent animosities and further hurt!*
- *I want to overcome misconceptions!*
- *I want to avoid misinterpretations!*

- *I want a chance to show my talents!*
- *I want to be loved!*
- *I want to be attractive to others!*
- *I want others to accept my point of view!*
- *I want to establish why people see me as they do!*
- *I want to be recognized as a leader in my field!*
- *I want to be able to exert a degree of control over others!*

Let's face it! If you're a normal, red-blooded American you want recognition. Your product *has* to have recognition. To sustain your ego-balance as well as your bank account you need this recognition every day of your life. You want the good image and why not?

The more outstanding your image, the greater becomes your spread of influence, the greater your success. You're building a "rep." You're developing the personality which others see. If that image breaks down in the public eye you lose stature. You lose goodwill. Prejudice builds up against you.

How can the matter be handled?

Try this on for size:

1. Every person seeking a place in the sun has to get himself into a position where he can command attention that is favorable.

2. He has to keep other people well-informed about his activities.

3. He has to be helpfully cooperative and useful. He should be community-conscious and aid others.

4. He has to capture public imagination and win public support to effectively get favorable reactions designed to help him in his reach for fame.

5. He has to handle people diplomatically and show his social and commercial muscle even while hiding his weaknesses and preventing additional errors of judgment.

You too can handle this P/R matter in the same manner. You too can make the most out of human relationships. You too can be a success by learning to communicate.

What Communication Means
To You In The P/R Program

The moment you convey any kind of idea or meaning you are communicating. You are "getting through" to someone. When you learn the words and the music which people like to hear you are on your way to being a more personable, a more vital human being.

> *How well you tie your process of communication to every desire for security, for power, skill, affection and love, knowledge, or even for mental and physical well-being, determines your personal success!*

The point is that YOU personally HAVE TO INFLUENCE HUMAN BEHAVIOR around you. How? Here are some grass-root tips on how to get at people where they live:

How to Get the Most
Out of Human Relationships

1. *Let people know that you care*
   Admire them publicly. TELL THEM you think they are great and in due time they will think the same about you. Through praise and admiration, lay the foundation for building a career.

2. *Demonstrate that you are a personable and desirable friend*

   ACT friendly. BE friendly. Talk it up and SHOW it!

3. *Agree with people*

   Reassure people. Confirm their opinions about themselves. Tell them they are right. Later you can persuade them otherwise.

4. *Use flattery—it WILL get you somewhere*

People feed on adulation. They need it just like you need it. So play to the house. Build their egos. Create that invigorating impulse that people feel when they are pleased.

5. *Present new ideas slowly*

New interests and new attitudes should be introduced very slowly. Never rupture status quo. Make people susceptible to new ideas. Plant them. Create a need, a demand. When the idea grows, capitalize on it!

6. *Take advantage of current ideas*

When a law, or attitude exists that you can take advantage of, TAKE IT! Ride it if it is beneficial to you and causes no one else harm. Develop it! Advertise it! Give it the good word.

7. *Avoid conflict*

Nothing destroys rapport faster than conflict. Walk away from trouble unless you are involved in something highly personal. Then jump in with both feet.

8. *Learn to sound out what other people dislike*

Avoid common disapproval. KNOW WHAT PEOPLE DON'T WANT. If they are critical, beware. The pot is boiling and there's no profit in being the one who gets boiled.

9. *Never rely on guesswork*

Research everything. Have the facts and nothing but the facts if you would be closer to right in controlling people.

10. *Establish a favorable image of yourself*

Once the good image is established maintain it!

When you learn to satisfy human urgencies, needs, and wants, you are on your way to talking your way to success with people. When you learn to develop NEW WANTS in others, you have already become a public relations specialist. You have advanced to the point where you are using words as the vehicle to the Promised Land.

Your personal P/R program is power-packed

If you would gain stature in your business, your profession, your church or society, if you would command respect, if you would use the power-pack of P/R to gain cooperation, all you have to do in manipulating words and action, is to make them demonstrate *courage, persistence, tact, and objectivity.*

If you would take advantage of this power-packed package called personal public relations, then you must coordinate and correlate your personal qualifications with the qualifications and needs of those around you.

This means YOU HAVE TO KNOW PEOPLE! You have to know what makes them tick. The moment you begin to pluck the heartstrings of humanity, and help people to formulate a policy that will bring them gain, or appease their conscience, you are on your way to fame. You will have motivated them to action!

When you develop the know-how that brings them understanding, cooperation and goodwill YOU ARE DOING A SELLING JOB! You are a Harry Jacobsen at *Gentleman Jim's* greeting customers at the door with "Hello, Senator!"

Develop this know-how! Convert it to do-how! Prevent mistakes that can hurt you.

You can't please everyone

Even if you can't please everyone, try to understand those whom you can't reach through your personal P/R program. Remember that others think differently than you do. They may see words in a different light than you do. What they hear you say may be misinterpreted. On their lips our words become something different. Public personages have this problem day after day.

"Public relations" means that
you walk and talk with people

Whether or not you further your career and build up Golden Goals through a personal public relations program depends on "getting through to people." You have to do it through words to be effective. To accomplish the objectives of success you have to use methods to get the results you want. Before you start to use the action-compelling methods you will find in the rest of this book you must ask some questions of yourself:

HUMAN RELATIONS
CHECK-OUT COUNTERS

Ask yourself the following:

1. *What actual attitudes do I want to develop in the people about me?*
2. *What personal image am I trying to develop?*
3. *Am I using the right medium in words to do it?*
4. *Are people grasping what I say?*
5. *Do they absorb and hold what I have written or said?*
6. *Am I getting through?*
7. *Am I at the level of their language comprehension so that they do not misunderstand?*

In other words, as you become totally aware of your personal contact with people you have to become aware that you have to *talk at their level.* You have to talk the language they understand!

When you are writing, write as you talk. When you talk, speak understandably, simply, and with force.

How to get better
results out of words

To get the best results out of words use short sentence structures and smaller words. Use names. Use personal references. Avoid complicated figures of speech. Avoid the abstract. Put your finger on the facts and point them out in brief. Do this consistently as you develop the tricks of the trade in building your personal P/R package. Use words! Use them efficiently! Use contrast! Use comparison! Use tact with your impact!

Remember that today is a day that demands more and more words of persuasion and power. Why? Today is a fantastic period of scientific, social and industrial churning. It's a booming turbulent change. All of it in a mad-paced expression of pseudo-knowledge and sophistication. All of it bustling and bristling, a tinsel and glitter world, all of it in the most amazingly awesome and confounding revolution ever to hit the world. All of it marking a magnificent boom and if you would jump on the bandwagon for a piece of the action, welcome aboard.

Where do you start?

Maybe you want to develop your P/R package as a real estate salesman and become fluent in vending plush housing in the suburbs. Maybe you want to get into the insurance game. Maybe you would like to be one of the "image makers" from Madison Avenue. Maybe you're interested in becoming an educator, a minister of the gospel, the warden of a prison. Maybe all you want is the gift-of-gab as you make a run for the girlies.

Whatever it is you want, you have to have the right words to do it. You have to have the training for it. You have to be able to develop the know-how that makes you more personable and acceptable. For this reason you have to develop your personal P/R package and make it live. You have to go all out with personal public relations if you would develop the *impression circle* around you that I call "Personality Appeal." You have to captivate and conquer!

3

The Aura Of Words In "Personality Appeal" And How Your "Impression Circle" Works

Personality, in all its uniqueness, is an intensely human mask used in the conscious effort to win people to you and achieve that place in the sun called "success." Personality controls success and for this there is no substitute. In all of its intimately friendly phases the radiance of words creates the sum total of what I prefer to call "Personality Appeal." It's an "Impression Circle" that makes you attractive.

O f what is the Impression Circle composed? How does Personality Appeal work? How are words used to create it? Whom
does it affect? Why develop it?

These are pertinent and necessary questions if you are ready
to believe and act on the premise that you can talk your way to
success with people. The answers you find in this book are equally
pertinent. Some you may think are impertinent as well because
they conflict with what you have thought in the past. To this I
say, "Good, let's go from there. Let's use the methods by which
you can see and evaluate yourself. Let's take the opportunity to
look into the mirror of self-appraisal and determine what your
course of action is going to be as you seek that place in the sun
that is rightfully yours."

Personality Appeal, A Public
Index Of Personal Qualifications

In brief, *"Personality Appeal"* is a person's index of qualifications for social, business or professional survival. It inventories the
contents of his bid for success. It is that which distinguishes one
person from another, his personal effort to achieve a goal by utilizing what he has and making the most of it.

What are the properties
of personality appeal?

PERSONALITY APPEAL IS:

 1. *Physical appearance*

    It is your voice, your hair, your posture, your ex-
    pression, your physique and your health. It is your
    personal charm which emanates from you with every
    word you make and every step you take to get through
    to people.

 2. *Emotional aspects*

    Enthusiasm and courage, love and hate, vivacity and
    sense of humor, all are factors which control the
    temperament and action you exhibit to others. You

are an ambivert, an introvert or an extrovert by your own doing and because of this, success is somethng that you alone can make.

3. *Intellectual level*

The man or woman who learns to reason and form judgments about himself, as well as about other people, is first to succeed. Out of his conscious demand for success he helps others and makes a dynamic response. He adjusts to people. He paves the way with the kind of words that indicate his intellectual level.

4. *Moral and spiritual plane*

The person who reaches for something greater than himself finds beauty and goodness in God, and in man. His concepts, ideals, friendships, and insights arrive automatically. From this comes the self-realization of his values in helping others. From the moral and spiritual plane comes courage, honesty, perseverance and conscientiousness. From it come powers culminating in that intangible sum total of individuality called *"character."*

5. *Social face*

You present your social face each day. It is your handshake, your sympathy, your tolerance, your ability in leading and guiding others. It is your adaptability to change as well as your ability to recognize the rights of others. It is your fairness, your ability, your tact.

6. *The sum total of desires*

Man does what he has to do in the face of everything else. It is his habits, his longings, his tastes and his interests that make him act this way. It is the will to serve others who need him most.

7. *Everything creating a bond between you and people*

The strength of this social bond is entirely dependent

upon your efforts to gain that desirable place of public recognition.

In other words, through the use of *Personality Appeal,* and the sight and sound of words that are a delicate part of all this, success is in your hands. You, indeed, are architect of your career. By the studied use, not abuse, of *Personality Appeal* and the power of words that shape it, you assure yourself of the Golden Goals as you talk your way to success with people.

Personality Appeal, or that *Impression Circle,* is not just charm. It's not just how you act, or how you appear. It is a master plan of many interlocking factors creating a particular aura which identifies you for what you are by what you do and say.

Approximately 85 per cent of what you say never registers, and when you are trying to get through to other people there is a communication lag. This lag is not always the other person's fault. Somewhere along the route you have failed to get through. You have failed to clarify the picture with the right words and actions. You have not used the language which the other person understands. You have not riveted his attention or gotten his co-operation from the start. *You have not made the other person WANT to listen.* Since you have not awakened response, and have not realized the dramatic necessity of using communication to put across your message, you lose the chance to win friends and influence people. You lose the lifeline to success.

Why learn the art of communication in personality appeal?

Success comes in direct ratio to the ability to understand people. People are controllable through words and can be drawn into the magic zone of your *Impression Circle.*

In today's way of life it becomes increasingly necessary to utilize communications, or other audio-visual means, as a method to dispel all the distractions which make people more and more resistant, more sophisticated, more impervious to inept forms of communcation.

People today are more educated. They are more blasé. They are less susceptible, for example, to propaganda which stipulates that doctors, as men-in-white, are next to godliness. The public today knows better.

As a result, a doctor must capture his patient's attention in order to retain him as a patient. He must do this by getting through to him, through the medium of words and actions called that *Impression Circle* in which he projects the idea that his patient is a V.I.P. . . . a very important patient . . . and not just a case history or a number in the file. As with physicians, this also pertains to you. It is necessary to learn the art of communication in *Personality Appeal* so that you can be attractive to them.

You have to attract others to make them want to hear what you have to say. You have to break through their preoccupation with their own problems and interests. Verbal communication thus becomes a social lever of understanding through conversation. As such it pries aside sophistication, preoccupation and stupidity. By impressing people, and holding their attention or interest they are persuaded to follow you.

Young or old, uneducated or Ph.D., all people need direction. They need to be persuaded. They need to be influenced. They need to feel secure and the depth of this need is constant. So is the need to appease it, and that's where talking your way to success begins.

The first duty to people, in your trek to success, is seeing them as individuals. To reach a person persuasively you have to get through to him at his level. You have to determine his emotional sensitivity spots and bandage his emotional injuries with words, words of sympathy, words of understanding, words of hope.

How you get through to people is accomplished through the art of communication. It is done through various methods of which the voice is one.

Your Voice . . . Passport To Success

As an indelible impression your voice is like a fingerprint. It leaves a tattletale impression day after day.

Although the average person doesn't realize it, *his voice is 15 per cent of his Personality Appeal.* By cultivation, his voice can become a finely tooled instrument for 100 per cent communication.

Remember that the human voice CAN be an instrument of

charm. It CAN be vocal magic surrounding anyone who uses it effectively to create his *Impression Circle*.

Your voice is a
persuasive power · . . use it!

An ugly voice turns people away as effectively as does a dirty body. Public relations status, and person-to-person relationships, are dependent upon the personality you present each day. Remember that your voice CAN be appealing. It CAN be persuasive if you utilize the unique power of using words to your advantage.

Your voice can be a stimulant. It can be a depressant, a hypnotic, or a press agent. It can calm people in pain or excite them. It can convince those who have a lot at stake to act against their better judgment. It can turn suggestion into command and elicit cooperation when all other efforts have failed. It can convert to action. *Your Voice can be your power!*

How does your voice
actually affect people?

Spoken words reveal attitudes. They spotlight a thought and the very tone of words may imply what words themselves do not say. Because 95 per cent of all human beings misuse their voices, they often say what they have to say in a manner they later regret. They misuse their voices and it is this misuse of tone, rather then content, which is so often misconstrued.

This means that a voice which is monotonous, lacks vitality, flows without end, is emotionless, carries negative inflections, or is scratchy or loud, is bound to be irritating to people. You simply don't get through when this happens.

No one can afford to be unconscious of the power and glory of the human voice in the bid for success. No one can afford to have people identify him through particularly irritating sounds.

If your voice is dull, people expect that you will be dull. If your voice is gravelly, rough or uncouth, people classify you as gravelly, rough or uncouth, and only the strongest of other personality facts in the *Impression Circle* can ever change this classification.

Because of this your voice can become a forbidding showcase

when improperly used. Or, it can become a glorious route to success with people. So your voice, as part of your *Personality Appeal,* and a living part of your *Impression Circle,* is essential to success.

As a guide to avoiding the kinds of speaking voices which antagonize people I have set up a chart indicating types of voices which people do not like. These are obnoxious vocal characteristics which hack holes in your *Impression Circle.*

ARE YOU HARMING YOUR
SUCCESS CHANCES
WITH AN IRRITATING VOICE?

The kinds of voices
which annoy people:

1. Apathetic voices
2. Booming voices
3. Emotionless voices
4. Gutteral voices
5. Harsh voices
6. Hissing voices
7. Loud voices
8. Monotonous voices
9. Nasal voices
10. Rapid-speaking voices
11. Scratchy voices
12. Shrill voices
13. Very soft voices
14. Voices begging sympathy and whining
15. Voices filled with poor grammar
16. Voices filled with slang and profanity
17. Voices without articulation
18. Voices without breath control
19. Voices with downward inflections
20. Words interspersed by gulping, smoking, eating, blowing, and so forth.

People become appeased, angry, gentle, or violent, according to the sound of words. Through words they are motivated to act and react, and a person's enthusiasm for you and his attentiveness to what you are saying is keyed to the right use of words. There must be no distractions, no social static, to irritate the people with whom you would be a success.

Loyalty is born and conceived in words

Loyalty is certainly born and conceived in what you say and do each day. It may wither away the same way. *Loyalty lives or dies in accordance with how well you tell a person what he wants to hear.* Through words, a doctor may stimulate a patient to recovery. Words ineptly said may trigger an emotional explosion that leads to that patient's untimely death. As such, words are powerful medicine. As such they are the bridge between doctor and patient and over this bridge the patient should be led to move without fear.

All people react to words. The advertiser buying radio and TV time, the clothes buyer listening to the designer's pitch, the Avon lady at the door. No one is immune to words because words can be weapons or olive branches. They can hold promise for the future or they can hold hell.

Use the wrong words and everything that makes a person what he is vomits up out of his hereditary background. All of his past, his stored-up attitudes, his fears, either crush him or fortify him in accordance with the type of individual he is, and it is your necessity to know and understand people and the influence of words upon them. It is your necessity to develop a million-dollar personality so that your *Personality Appeal* is magnetically strong. Your *Impression Circle* should be developed so that you draw people into the aura of your persuasion.

Develop that human mask. Use it. Win people to you as you use words to talk your way to success. Develop the art of the "snow job" and watch words pay.

4

There's No Business Like "Snow" Business

A *"snow job" is the art of lying and smiling at the same time . . . a way of squeezing information into acceptable forms, a technique for using words shaped to fit a purpose and convert the ridiculous to the sublime. A "snow job" may be used to camouflage mediocrity or camouflage the truth. It may be used to make a good thing look even better.*

Public relations specialist Alan Harrington* defines P/R (public relations) as "the craft of arranging truths so that people like you." In other words, when you use words in a "snow job" you are altering truth just enough to make your product look good.

Gutsy press agentry pays!

Personality, like public relations, is the softsell with a gutsy and knowledgeable program behind it. It's a *snow job* that can be applied on massive corporations seeking the Good Guy Image or on politicians seeking a place in the political sun. It can be used on developing a new face for an old product or for whitewashing a gangster who's gone under the cover of "going legit."

It's true that the *snow job* is designed to please others and phase them into sleep-walking. But in developing your own personality approach, your own *Impression Circle,* and selling yourself as you step up to success, you have to create your own *Good Guy Image.* You have to create an acceptable and admirable façade. You have to contourize your life and maintain goodwill toward you. You have to do this with purpose and intent if you would get your Golden Goals. You HAVE to be gutsy! Your *snow job* has to have purpose and you can't be meek about it at any time. The meek will never inherit the earth. They can't! They have no drive, no urgency, no inspiration, no objectives!

"Know your objectives long in advance," advises P/R specialist Mel James. "Create the right personal image. Build it. Develop pretty pictures, pretty patterns of words and slogans, but most of all be prepared to change everything at a moment's notice when the going gets rough."

In your use of words to create your public image, James suggests that you set up a personal chart that symbolizes YOUR *Good Guy Image.*

On first impact these images may sound like Pollyanna Night at the Bijou. They will sound artificial and they are! So admit it. But here's the point! *Good Guy Images* are publicly accepted! These are the images by which people live. These are the images

---

* Alan Harrington, *Life in a Crystal Palace* (New York: Alfred Knopf, 1959), p. 210.

you develop with words and action as you talk your way to success with people. Stray from these accepted patterns and you become the villain in the piece.

"GOOD GUY" IMAGERY
TO GET PUBLICLY ACCEPTED

In essence, your personality
and P/R program should shout:

* I am pure. I am Sir Galahad on a white steed.
* Lean on me. I am thy rod and thy staff.
* I am clean and I am good.
* I represent hard work and achievement.
* I move where angels fear to tread. I'm strong.
* I willingly help others in distress.
* My capabilities are at your service.
* I help people to achieve happiness and success.
* I'm honest. I admit when I'm wrong.
* I provide a strong example to follow.
* I am happy and nice to be near.
* I will get along famously with you.
* I understand you and your problems.
* I am respectful and courteous.
* I am socially conscious and broadminded.
* I know my job and am competent.
* I want you to have the best.
* _____
* _____
* _____
* _____
* _____

NOTE: *Fill in additional "Good Guy Images" you would like to portray. Make your own list of what you would like to be and how you would present yourself in public.*

The Lone Ranger rides again!

In creating your image, always portray good against evil. Wave the "good guy" banners in your mind until you are sold on the theme. Then wave them in public. Even while you are doing this, beware of riding through the gopher holes of a *snow job*. You may break a leg in a trap of your own making, as any good P/R specialist will tell you.

Can your "snow jobs" be booby-trapped?

You can't be Sir Galahad all the time. Sometimes you get dirt on your armor. Even the judicious use of mouthwash and armpit deodorant doesn't always do the trick. The booby trap, then, is in the words you use, the unsocial words, which you should recognize and know.

Prepare an offensive defense against social booby traps and be ready to face challenge as you work your way up to success. Be ready to wash that gnawing feeling of inadequacy out of your life. Be strong by making yourself strong. Build your "snow" business and make it click.

It's nice promoting others into prominence all the time, but do some of it on yourself. Give yourself one of those "snow jobs." Remember that the armor of Sir Galahad was great for knights of old, but what modern lady will spend the night with a tin man?

Be human. Admit your weaknesses. Then bury them! Develop the façade that makes you attractive to people. Pull them into your *Impression Circle* and never permit yourself to be lost in the shadow of others.

It's true that a successful P/R man is often lost in the shadow of those for whom he plans and ghost-writes. I know this. For years I witnessed this happening to me. As a voice behind the scenes I guided and directed others to their particular thrones. For years I hid successfully behind a façade even while helping others up the Glory Trail and you can spend a lifetime lost in obscurity if you desire. You can live and die on Obscurity Street, but I made up my mind that this was not for me.

Today I say do a *snow job* on yourself! If you are going to step up to success through words, remember there's no business like "snow" business! You're in the spotlight! You're the feature performer!

Crusty thinking? Gutsy? Indeed it is! It's the kind of thinking that comes with the realization that success is not a natural phenomenon. It's not something you inherit. It's something you create! It's something you do! It's everything you say!

Why not be noticed socially? Why not make things happen in your social environment? Why not become a skyrocket attention-getter in your professional, business or industrial world? Why not move in on your objectives with good, solid planning. Ghost-write your own material. USE it! Use the right words, the right phrases, the right slogans with the right actions at the right time! Move gracefully through public life and dance to the melody of social acceptance with you beating out the tempo. Fabricate your program in advance. KNOW where you want to go. Then GO!

Develop your plan-of-action
long in advance

Before you do it, establish how you are going to act and what you are going to say. Create the scenario. Act it out in advance. Plan your program of operations and then move on your objectives. Publicize your message of individuality. Appeal to goodness in others as well as in yourself as you develop your *Good Guy Image.* Bring out their best by exemplifying your own. Create a star to follow and they will follow. They will be attracted. They will be drawn into the radiant network of your *Impression Circle.* You will engulf them with your million-dollar personality and become the success you want to be.

Sure, this is a hardnosed approach to the success game, but the very fact that you realize there is a need for a *snow job* indicates that you are conscious of developing and planning in advance a plan-of-action that will help you win friends and influence people. Your personal *snow job,* through words as well as action, indicates you are conscious that you need a public relations program. Whether it is an artificial image or not, create YOUR *Good Guy Image.* Whether it is all a lie at this moment is immaterial, because as you begin to practice it, this is what you will be! What really matters is that you fit the *Good Guy Images* by which other people live.

The very fact that you want to develop that image called a *"million-dollar personality"** already indicates your need for a *snow job*. It's a tacit admission that you want to get through to people, that you want to use every means to put yourself across. It indicates a need for the veneer of a personal public relations program and using the right words to help you on your way to success.

The need for a *Good Guy Image* indicates you are becoming aware of what other people think, and the need to be seen by them in the light of what they understand and desire. It indicates an awareness of the necessity to be prepared against failure as well as the unexpected. It indicates you are moving forward with new thoughts, new concepts and that you are going to take directional control of your life from here on in with the forward thrust of words that can talk you up to success.

Even while admitting that the approach to people is often artificial, remember that the baby's cry gets results. The baby puts on a show until he gets action. He does this by appealing to emotions and to love. He uses his voice to do it and you can use your voice the same way.

In planning a procedure for publicizing yourself, here are some strategic phases to follow as you develop the kind of *snow job* that you can use as you talk your way to success with people.

STEP-BY-STEP ROUTINE
FOR PERSONALIZING
YOUR "SNOW JOB"

1. *Coordinate your "snow job" with the interests of others.*

2. *When you see opportunity, walk and talk your way right into it.*

3. *Pre-plan all procedures to accomplish an objective.* Lay out the details. Know in advance your approach. Then be prepared to deviate a little. Keep flexible.

---

* J. V. Cerney, *How to Develop a Million-Dollar Personality* (West Nyack, N.Y.: Parker Publishing Co., 1964).

4. *Do a dry run on your prospective routine.*
Imagine it, create it, act it out in private before you try your performance in public.

5. *Notate how long each phase takes.*
Since everyone is keyed to time, KNOW how long your little act takes. Know what you can clip from your performance. Then punch across your message in the time you have.

6. *Say "Thanks" to those who help you.*

7. *Make allowances for things that can go wrong.*
Time is a major element, so allow for emergencies. Be prepared to change course on a moment's notice. Have ideas or objects ready to act as "fills" or substitutes.

8. *Set key dates for accomplishments.*
NAME your goals. Anchor them with dates.

9. *If an idea backfires, don't cry over it!*
Drop it dead. Set another idea into motion.

10. *If you can't say something good about someone or something in your P/R "snow job," say nothing at all.*
The same applies about yourself.

11. *Never overplay your role.*
Never give anyone opportunity to become suspicious of your *snow job*. Don't make it so obvious that it inspires distrust. Don't ever let anyone see you as being artificial.

12. *Maintain the "Good Guy Image" in public at all times even though it hurts.*
Even though people are rupturing your serenity with nastiness, maintain your *Impression Circle*. Smile till your face cracks. When you get home you can strip the mask and let your distress out.

Pathway To Power
Through Speech

To be a dynamic organizer, to be publicly attractive, to be an outstanding salesman, public speaker or stage personality, you have to have not just a voice but the facility of speech. You have to know how to project yourself across to other people as you apply your *snow job*. Your speaking voice should be so vibrantly concise that an image is formed in the minds of those who hear you.

> *Images are built with words. The words must be specific, concise, dramatic, colorful and compelling. They must have urgency and motion. They should flow easily and with purpose. They should create more than a vague impression.*

Speaking clearly to get a message across is a vital necessity. *You have to make people understand!* I remember a patient of mine who came to the office one day and said her husband would not return.

"What did you say to him?" she wanted to know.

"All I said," I explained, "was that if he contined to mistreat you I was going to *castigate him.*"

"Oh, my god!" she gasped. "He thought you said you were going to castrate him!"

How to use
descriptive language

People imaginatively reinterpret that which you are saying. Because of this you have to dramatize what you say in terms of pictures they understand. This means you have to dramatize speech not just with inflection but by the picture inspired by what you say. So be impressive. Be spectacular if necessary, but put it across. Use photogenic words as you speak, but make them plain.

For example, if you are a grocer, don't just say, "These are good potatoes." Say, "These are Idahos. They're the best bakers. They melt in your mouth." If you are a car salesman don't say. "This car has eight cylinders." Instead say, "Here's power at your command!"

Appeal to wants and desires. Let other people see themselves in a relished position. Help them fulfill their ambitions by emphasizing their needs. Do the same for yourself, because it's all part of the *snow job*.

Persuasiveness with people
is an acquired characteristic

Adeptness in handling people with words comes only with training. It comes with learning what to do and how to say it. You are not born with this capacity. It comes with time and experience. Because of this, *the persuasiveness which influences people is an acquired characteristic.*

Admittedly the capacity to lower social barriers and persuade others, through language, takes training. It takes education. Quite often it is a comedy of errors before you become adept in its use. Since the art of persuasion is not inherited it becomes increasingly necessary to achieve the abilities to get the job done. Words have to be coordinated with action. The social finesse has to be developed.

Let's put it this way—"No product sells itself." *You* are a product. YOU are a social product and you, like many a good product, languish in a warehouse because no one is doing a selling job. No one is giving the right sales talk. No one is doing a *snow job.*

Whether you are selling your *Good Guy Image,* rubber goods, or chemicals by the ton, you have to learn the methods for making a solid sales pitch. You have to learn the presentation that makes you personable.

The "pitch" is the sales talk you give to attract and focus attention. It is your method of wheeling and dealing with terminology that stimulates wants and needs, words that appeal to someone's pride or sense of humor. It means getting others to do what you want them to do without confusing or hurting them or interfering with their way of life.

In this technique you sell the coffee's aroma and taste and not the bean or grind. You sell the sexy look, the potential of romance on a sandy shore, the possibility of becoming a millionaire by buying a swatch of uranium stock. It's all a *snow job* and you're just the one who can do it!

It's all there—appealing to the big want, the fireball of desire, the appeal to pride, to vanity, to possession. You appeal to temptation and make it pay.

Design your personality pitch
to earn bigger payoffs

The big self-sell, in creating your personal *snow job*, has to be designed to yield a handsome payoff. It's the hotline proposition with the fringe benefits of personal satisfaction, the super-salesmanship of words.

One day in a New York art gallery I watched and listened to a sales person. He worked his client into position for the "hook" and it was fascinating to see him puff the man up with a personality pitch before he capped the deal. It was a *snow job* all the way and here's the slice of life I witnessed:

"This isn't just a canvas, Mr. Big," said the salesman earnestly. "This painting isn't just oil and a frame. It's a Rembrandt! A masterpiece! Only an extraordinary man like yourself could own it!"

To all this Mr. Big said nothing. He pursed his lips, cocked his head from side to side. In the dim light his spectacles were dull dual headlights peering through the underlit gallery as the salesman's voice went on.

"This painting was part of Maeterlinck's collection before he fled the Nazi invasion. It was twice stolen by international thieves. Once it contributed to the death of lovers. An amazing history, Mr. Big, but the man who buys this Rembrandt buys more than history. He buys mystery and a million dollars' worth of notoriety. He buys affluence and fame already built in. He buys a tremendously valuable possession. Shall I have Brinks deliver it to your home by armored car?"

Use Words to get
at people's emotions

There are certain basic elements in all people which you can twist with words.

Let's look at the entire matter coldly and calmly for the results that we want to achieve—notably, talking our way to success with people. Emotions control people. People with internal conflicts, for example, panic readily. People with preconceived opinions and ideas often act without reason. Yell "fire!" and they run nude from their bedrooms.

Those who lack self-confidence, those who worry or are insecure, have phobias or live in fear, those who are religious or fatalistic, will yield readily to the powerful influence of dramatic and descriptive words.

A memorable example was the incident of the men from Mars landing in the United States. It was the evening of October 30, 1938. Mercury Theatre and Orson Welles were presenting H. G. Wells's *War of the Worlds*. Dramatically, emphatically, in newscaster style, the Martians were presented as having landed in New Jersey. They had knocked off the National Guard and were taking over. The effect of the broadcast was electric.

Monstrous panic spread through the United States. People actually believed what they had heard. They didn't stop to verify that it was "only a radio show," that it was just words. Instead those "words" got at their basic fears, words that touched their emotions in a time of change (1938) in the world: depression, tension, pending war. People were ripe for panic. They were ripe for the sensationalism of Orson Welles's dramatic presentation. They were stirred to desperation that night when the fictitious Martians came. They were ready to explode emotionally and they did.

With words you too can "stir men's souls." You too can pull the stops on standard everyday crises by triggering the loyalties of people as well as triggering their fears. In so doing you develop strong personal indentification. You develop a successful route to people through words.

To create YOUR personal success through words identify yourself with race, religion, class, product, talent or concept. Establish indentification to get mass action. Stimulate that something in people that makes them act. Pinch their socially sensitive areas to get them to do what you would like them to do. Use words to help others identify themselves as *Good Guys* through charity or other forms of giving. Let them identify with you. If you would be a winner and inherit the good things on this earth, be inspiring!

The meek will never inherit the earth

The meek *can't* inherit the earth because they have nothing that impels them to success. They have no moxie, no know-how, no place to go. They don't know how to do a *snow job* on themselves or anyone else if they tried. As a result success seldom comes to the timid. The meek have neither the tempo, the structure, the urgency, the drive or the stride to get the earth. Their public relations and *Good Guy Images* are nil.

Success takes guts. It takes that educated something slangily referred to as *moxie* or know-how. But it takes more than that. It takes *do-how* to ride the crest of survival. It takes the Big Push in moving up off Obscurity Street to the Golden Goals and the Golden Gains of achievement.

It takes going after the status symbols with tough-minded insistency. It takes action!

Since you do not belong to the meek there is neither time nor space in your life to bleed back into the Sargasso Sea of apathy. Obscurity Street overflows with the meek and the nobodies and there's no room for you there. In fact, you don't want room there. You want to move on out!

To get out of the self-formed traps it takes controlled action. It takes forward-thrust and the ability of persuasion. It takes the rhythm of personal motivation that urges people to prominence.

You are the key in career control

In a thousand different ways success comes by way of the "hard and soft sell" of words. It comes with stirring up desires and controlling urgencies until they become volatile expressions that are persuasive and lasting. Most of all, the key, in achieving success and career control, is YOU!

> *There can be no success without you. YOU create your own success! Only YOU can remodel your personality and your life. Only YOU can reap the Golden Gains of the more opulent life by using verbal expressions necessary to get the job done. There are many such expressions, many such words, and all of them are wrapped up in YOU!*

Be constantly reminded that words are image-makers, formulators of invention, convention and motivation. They are triggers for emotion, driving powers for persuasion and molification and sub-jugation and propaganda. Words are public relations symbols packaged for a *snow job,* magic action-packed articulations—both oral and written—that can be said with charm, with gentility, with refinement, or they can be destructive with the negatives of hostil-ity, anger and verbal fire. Words can tell the story of bitter de-nunciation, hatred, torture and the vomitus of blood-and-guts living which the meek cannot stand. It takes this verbal know-how and if you have the educated urgency for success, you can compete anywhere under any circumstance and win!

Language is a
volatile expression

When you use words you use a method of expression. The small-est word, in the proper manner, can be amplified with innuendo. One tiny word may destroy a million-dollar deal or blow a court case sky high. One little word can bring about murder or destroy a marriage. One word can destroy a nation, and these are the nega-tives of terminology, the destructive aspects of words.

On the positive side, however, there is an even greater power. One sentence, one selling title, an attention-getting phrase may bring a fortune. The words "I love you" have created worlds of happiness and togetherness for many. The Ten Commandments encapsulate ten great powers. Words may bring the world to your doorstep as you advertise the greatest mousetrap.

So why not USE WORDS?

Why not use words for the big win? Why not use them to reach out for recognition? Why not reach for the status symbols through their magic power and leave Obscurity Street behind? Why not do a *snow job* on yourself as well as others and seek success?

Move up! Move up through self-persuasion. Use the explosive dramatics of words to sell yourself into the realm of better living. Develop the ability to encourage people to react on your behalf, to do what you want

*them to do, to have them act! Develop specialized skills
with words to draw people to you. Make your "Impression Circle" desirable. Make yourself indispensable as
a specialist with a specialized skill.*

SEVEN REMINDERS ABOUT
BUILDING YOUR "SNOW BUSINESS"

Key action for the smart set:

1. *Maintain your personal importance*

   Remain in the middle of things and never retreat.
   Learn to gauge yourself and gauge others. Sound
   them out on what they think and feel. Then lead
   them down persuasive channels that you personally
   prepare.

2. *Learn to put on the pressure without being obvious*

   Learn to overcome the fears of others. Learn to overcome their inertia, and their suspicions. Capitalize
   on their pride, their jealousies and even on their in-
   competence by putting the pressure on without their
   knowing it.

3. *Probe humanity for its weaknesses*

   Recognize the soft spots in human nature that provide psychological wedges where you can move in,
   areas where you can insert yourself into their lives
   and get through to them! Penetrate their trigger
   zones! Reach them! Learn the basic motives that propel people to do what they do. Work the angles for
   all you can get!

Cold-blooded? Oh no! I'm talking about real red-blooded success items. I'm talking about the intestines of achievement and why
the meek will never inherit the earth. I'm talking about the things
upon which you have to capitalize if you would become persuasive
and make part of this world yours.

4. *Know the greeds of men!*

Know the larceny that stirs in their souls. Understand their vanity, their avarice, and interest in self. Know how to *appeal to wants, desires for pleasure, and convenience. Appeal to basic laziness and all other social defects* that they may possess. *Get through to them in their language! They must understand!*

5. *Know their loves, their kindnesses, their need for happiness*

Men need to have their vanity fed but they also need to be loved, to be cherished, to have security with someone who counts to them. Your first move then is to become conscious of the fact that *people are interested only in themselves.* They come first, not you, and from here on in you have to believe this so strongly that you build up the emotional steam that will make you less conscious of your old limited concepts.

The moment you recognize the opportunities for success that knowing people provides, you can insert yourself into their lives. The moment you recognize that you have to screen out your own ego from where you have kept it smothered, you begin your success drive.

6. *Let others strut and puff—Compliment them.*

So what does it cost you? What do words cost? Nothing! So cover people with glory! Shower them with honors! Give them praise! Give them sympathetic audience as they show off for your viewing. Let them parade. Let them have their moment. Then, step in and take over when the moment is ripe!

It's true! There's no business like "snow" business and nothing that creates such an impression as a warm and sincere *snow job.* It doesn't have to be an artifice. It doesn't have to be a lie. You can practice it until it becomes habit, and the moment it becomes habit so that your *snow job* is constantly on display you are on your way to success. You have begun to make your personal P/R program pay.

Of course it's all front! Of course it's social seduction! Of course it's a *snow job*. But like personality, it's the front you need if you would develop words, and the end results of words, into a formula for success!

5

Developing
The Oral Formula
For Success

The hotline of words to people is not without hazard because of the emotional attachment of words. Words have different meanings to different people. How you look at and listen to words may change as your understanding grows. But more than this, there is something else you can use as you reach for success. It's a formula and a technique that makes words profitable.

49

Words are meaningless until put to use. So are formulae. In all cases they have to be transposed to mental or physical action to make them come alive or put across a point.

Like the farmer who hit his mule on the head with a club—"The fust thing in gitting him to work is to git his attention."

> *Remember that thought and emotion in the brain are words reduced to silence. Words which go unused are silence. Prayers, joys, and anguish are silence until they break through and become heard. WORDS HAVE TO BE EXPRESSED. They have to be said. They have to be shouted, crooned and cried out. They were born to become action and if you would develop YOUR FORMULA FOR SUCCESS you have to set words into motion.*

It's true that not all emotions are reducible to words. Tenderness is a physical expression. Words too often are inadequate in expressing feelings or emotions. Pain and suffering are physical and this no words can explain.

Happiness is expression. So is delight. So is love, and each is a hidden persuader, a powerful formulator for action, each an ingredient in the formula for achieving better living, each a catalyst that makes you walk tall and think big every day of your life, each designed to help you think rich, to think success, and reach for it . . . if you use the right words.

How effectively you use these human forces, these power-encapsulated dynamos called emotions, and the words which well from them, predetermines the personality you show. It focuses the spotlight on the growth of your image of success.

The Silent Senses
Play a Coy Role in
The Trek to Success

Since we live by words and symbols, the words and symbols themselves determine our areas of aspiration. They determine our goals. They determine hopes and interests.

"An interest," said John Dewey, "is an activity that springs from need and moves in the direction of a goal that is calculated to satisfy that need."*

As you move toward your goals your needs impel you to act, react and abreact in characteristic ways. Your wants and your needs convert to feelings and emotions first in the chemistry of silence. Finally they reach such strength that they break through their shell just as does the maturing ovum break through the shell of the female ovary. Then it prepares for pregnancy and finalization of possible concept in moving into position where urges are converted to action. Words take over. The idea is born.

Let's open this package: In converting *your* feelings and emotions about success into words, have you as yet broken through to action? Have you started to use words as your route to success? Have you channeled thought and desire into the vital terminology of "drive"? Those deep deep urgencies for success that you have experienced— have they led you to *act?* Have those silent senses manipulated you into physical action to achieve? If they have, then aid and abet them. Let them do it, because this is your word-approach to success.

The silent senses impel all of us toward goals. They promote needs. You NEED! You WANT! You DO! It's as simple as that. When you want something you go after it. Power begins in the words that stimulate and success comes when you have a formula that converts that which is already in you into the externalization of achievement. It converts it into goals.

How do you know the goal you have chosen is right?

To forecast your future success through the leverage of words ask yourself: "What interests me most? What do I do best in my life from day to day? What makes me most happy?"

---

* John Dewey, "Theory of Valuation," *International Encyclopedia of Unified Science,* Vol. II, No. 4. (Chicago: University of Chicago Press, July 1939), pp. 17-66.

When you have answered these personal questions honestly and completely you will have brought into view a significant signpost. Suddenly you will be seeing and remembering a lot of unhappy people who are dissatisfied with their way of life. You will be looking down the road a piece to see cities full of them, millions of people gainfully employed, working where they are not happy, where they will be nothing but mediocre the rest of their lives, millions at jobs in which they have no true interest, additional millions who will never reach top performance because they lack a formula for success, a reason for being. They lack the will to achieve!

These are the unhappy, the dissatisfied, the disgruntled. These are the people who go out on "strikes." These are the Gray People of Obscurity Street who will forever remain obscure. They are the emotionally tired, the sad who have lost mobility. They have lost capacity or desire to communicate. In their self-imposed gray world they have become disinterested because they have no defined route to travel, no reason for living and loving, no formula for tomorrow or even for today.

Then what's the answer?

To help you determine whether the goal you have chosen is right fill in the following questionnaire. Start out now to pinpoint that which you would like to do most. (Leave sex out of the picture.) The moment you get that answer you can start designing your own formula for success.

SELF-INTEREST DEPTH PENETRANTS

What interests me most? _____

What do I do best? _____
What makes me happy? _____

Am I working at it now? _____ Yes
_____ No

Do I find pleasure in it
day after day? _____ Yes
_____ No

Am I happy going back
   to work each morning?_____Yes
                          _____No

Have I set a goal toward
   which to work?   _____Yes
                          _____No

Is my current job a forward
   step to the success I
   desire?   _____Yes
                          _____No

These are simple questions of self-interest. They help you penetrate your emotions and your thinking and touch on points of
motivation. They touch lightly on your needs, your goals, and your
actions. Each factor is a persuasive agent that not only indicates
the possibility of success in the future but predicts success itself.
Each lays down a forecast of your future. In these "depth pene-
trants" lies your tomorrow, because as words they are harbingers
of your future. They are the first symbols necessary in developing
that formula for success.

Self-concepts emerge
from self-understanding

By understanding yourself, and what holds your interest, you
learn to understand others so that you can give them, as well as
yourself, *directional control*. You judge their needs, their desires,
their reach for happiness and success by your own. You judge them
by your standards as well as by theirs. You use words to activate
them as well as inform them. You persuade them to action!

In trying to understand yourself you develop a self-concept. In
your own mind you create a desirable image and this is a valuable
focus of attention. From this focal point radiate concentric circles
called *communication* and *million-dollar personality* and *Impression Circle*. As a focal point you begin to move through environment smoothly or violently, in direct proportion to your ability
to get through to people and control yourself. You join forces with
people and environment and they become a part of you. It is here,

as Gardner Murphy points out, that "world and self flow into one another."*

The big factor here of which you have to take fullest advantage is that since you are a personality, and since you are a radiant focus of power transmission, as well as being an absorbent body, and since you are a receiving as well as a sending set, you can take advantage of your prime focal position.

As Far As You Are Concerned, You Are The Center Of The World!

College professor John Correlly says: "Why shouldn't you be the center of your part of the world? The world begins and ends with you because it does not exist if you do not exist to see it. Your world begins with your birth. It ends with your demise. It's that period in between when you achieve your success."

While you live you are a transmitter of energy that feeds out personal messages. These messages usually stem from want and need. They come from deep down urgencies within yourself. The biggest want of all is the want for success and the moment you learn to talk you learn to transmit words that will help you gain this end. You develop the ability to broadcast. In other words you learn to communicate through words. You beam a personal force in given directions to make your wants materialize.

In making this new magic, this generating source, come awake you create that which I call the *forward thrust* of word-power. This power needs guidance. It needs control. In doing this you begin to move into the future. You start learning to operate your self-generator and "turn it on" so that you not only can use your natural resources but can enlist the power sources of other people around you. It's here that the sensational magic of words plays its amazing and fabulous role!

*Force now takes on a
new character*

As an electromagnetic agent you radiate. As a human sending and receiving set, there radiates from you words, emotions, actions.

---
* Gardner Murphy, "Toward a Field Theory of Communication," *The Journal of Communication,* Vol. II, No. 4 (December, 1961), pp. 196-204.

Around you develops that *Impression Circle,* that *million-dollar personality,* that aura of significant influence.

Call this aura "charm," call it "air of command," call it "dominaton" or "hypnotic control." Call it *Personality Appeal,* but there it is! Power! Personality which radiates outwardly as you program yourself and your skills toward the Golden Goals of desire. You program yourself for the future and no one and nothing can stop you as long as you keep yourself under control. No one can stop you if you have a *formula for success* that you are putting into action!

Is there such a formula?

On this page, and those that follow, you will find a dynamic and forceful formula. It's yours for the using. It's encapsulated in five powerful words . . . five words that predict your future.

YOUR FORMULA FOR SUCCESS

**Five words that
master your destiny:**

FORWARD THRUST + DIRECTIONAL CONTROL = GOAL

**Let's reword that formula now.
Put it this way:**

EDUCATED ACTION + CAPABLE GUIDANCE = SUCCESS

FIVE WORDS! Five little words master your destiny! Five words of strength, words of impetus and intensity of effect, words of might and insight, compelling and compulsive forces that channel you to distinction and fame!

Do you already know how to use words to propel yourself to distinction? Can you use words graciously to create success? Can you use them to become a social, political or industrial power?

I say you CAN! I say you CAN become a success and a power in your own right. You have within you the mechanism that can make you great! You have only to utilize this magnificent word power to get through to people to achieve those Golden Goals you desire.

Professor Correlly asks: "What makes a great statesman? Is it action? No, it's words. Words create the actions of success which follow. What makes great diplomats greater? Words! What makes great politicians? Through what medium do the world's greatest writers reach success? Through the centuries what major vehicle has sustained the religions of the world? Of what are the annals of experiment and science full?"

All men, at all times, on all occasions have one thing in common—words! Words are the only medium of exchange stronger than money. They are the way to move from the lesser to the better, the way to move from Obscurity Street to Park Avenue, from Nobody Town to success, if you learn how to use them.

Take this formula for your own! Use it! Move into the future under complete control. Provide that *forward thrust!* Provide *directional control!* Provide the go-power that takes you to success!

Just exactly what happens through words?

Words are force in a capsule.

YOU are that capsule. As such, words are agents passing between yourself and other people. They may or may not convey a message. They may be directional or non-directional but in their passage they carry purpose. They are freighted with wants.

Look at it this way: When you talk to someone you are after something—food, a job, handling a big advertising account, a beautiful mate, a free flight to Nassau for a stretch in the sun, buying birth-control pills, taking the oral examination at the State Medical Board, jockeying the stock market with a news release to build for a kill—all done in words, words with purpose, words freighted with wants and premeditation.

Get accustomed to the idea that when you talk you are after something. When you say something it is shadowed by how and why you say it. No word, absolutely no word, is said without meaning and control. For this reason if you would develop your own personal power

through words, you might as well start right now to use
words with the calculated intent to succeed. Be coldly
frank in doing it!

Sometimes the words you and I use may cause you and me or
someone else grief. Words can be misunderstood and misinterpreted.
They may contribute to disaster, but that's par for the course.
There is no success that goes unmarked by failure along the way.

Behind every successful man is a trail of hurts and you
might as well resign yourself to this from the start as
you convert FORWARD THRUST + DIRECTIONAL
CONTROL into the goal you want. Educate your actions!
Guide them to assure the least possible number of com-
plications. Success, then, will be yours!

How do your words influence people?

The power of words over people is strong. They are strong because they convey the messages of want. Words, on impact, set up
reactions because words, and the tone and character in which they
are rendered, cause a typical response.

I divide these words of influence into rough categories. In their
effect on human beings they might be classified as (1) the *persuaders*, (2) the *informers*, (3) the *excitement-maintainers*, (4)
the *responders* or *achievers*.

The *persuaders* step up your adrenal glands and prepare you for
action. For example, say that you are a salesman and one of your
competitors says to you, "I just stole your Dumont account!" and
you are ready to beat the hell out of him.

The second group, the *informers*, prepare you for action through
understanding the situation of why something occurred or is about
to occur. By checking out the situation you learn why the competitive salesman took the account out from under your nose.

The third group, the *excitement-maintainers*, regulate and hold
the action steady. They keep it under control. You've recognized
where you flubbed on the account and now you begin to plot

out how you are going to win it back. You are building up the romance of competition. You're unsheathing your business and social claws. You're going back after that account tooth and nail. Maybe you're only clipping 10 per cent of a $700,000-a-year sale but it's yours. When you maintain your interest and excitement in your job you convert your job into a throughway to success and you use words in doing it all the way.

The fourth group, the *responders or achievers,* is an action-response, about which more will be said later. Let's give each now more specific identity.

The "Persuaders"
And How They Operate

The *persuaders* are dramatic words. As tools they come in two colors: one is harsh, the other is soft and gentle.

Harsh persuaders lay down rules and regulations with a heavy hand. They dedicate. They state unequivocally. They demand. They tell you or someone else what to do whether you want to do it or not. They cause you or someone else to act in a given manner. They create the first step in any pattern of response or behavior. They make the first step in developing susceptibility to command.

Soft persuaders are gentle. They encourage, tease, gently manipulate, diplomatically stimulate you into action. They influence thought. They convince. But beneath the velvet glove is steel and anyone interested in words as a powerful vehicle can gain success by manipulating humanity with the PERSUADERS. Words are the powerful vehicle with which to do it because they achieve results whether they are delivered with force or with deliberately quiet cunning. The *persuaders* can be your power.

The "Informers"
And How They Can Be Used

The *informers* identify and describe the scene. They are descriptive words: adjectives, adverbs, words of descriptive action. They are colorful words that identify and educate even as they set up the blueprint for your future. The *informer* words describe the situation. As descriptives they create the word picture of time, place, person or event. The *informers* are used to make a person understand a situation so that he can respond to it. He has to be told the who, what, when, where, why and how of it. By laying out specific knowledge such words not only inform you and others but stimulate an action-response. They get results!

The "Excitement-Maintainers" And Their Purpose

The purpose of the *excitement-maintainers* is to maintain a degree of excitement in an idea or a project. As an emotional booster shot they step up and maintain enthusiasm. They preserve or confirm an idea or thing. They affirm or assert something. They uphold, defend and vindicate. The *excitement-maintainers* are supportive agents when you need them most.

The "Responders" Or "Achievers" And Why They Are Vital To You

Words in this class make sure that one who responds to them is going to achieve a goal. These words direct the person toward a goal. They channel him to achievement. They keep an individual pointed toward accomplishment. The *achievers* have a follow-through that other words do not possess. They bring matters to a successful end. They are the words top salesmen use to close a deal. They're victory words that bring action to a head, boldness and ingenuity that indicates the overcoming of obstacles and discouragement. They mark the technique of that sales person in the New York art gallery who was doing a "snow job" on his millionaire client to sell him a Rembrandt.

Words expand your zone of influence

Through the vehicle of words is shaped persuasion. Words stir response. They stir up activity or imagination in one person but not in another. Words may develop trust or distrust, as do actions. Words may bring respect or disrespect, as do actions. Words may make others like or dislike you, so to win friends and clients you have to use the right words at the right time and make them believe it. You have to turn on your formula!

As your capability to persuade grows your *zone of influence* will grow. The objective therefore is to expand the resonse of people around you, to set up a program of command performance that controls them.

To achieve command of an area, or situation, no one can maintain morale or achieve love through using words of dominance and browbeating. No one can use words contributing to ridicule, sarcasm or socially debride the thin skin of humanity and not expect something adverse to happen. Because of this it is necessary to use the *persuaders.*

>   *Use persuader words not actually to manipulate people but to EXCITE THEM INTO WANTING TO MA- NIPULATE THEMSELVES INTO ACTION! These are the motivators about which we'll talk later, the key words in your Formula for Success.*

The magic of words can achieve your end

In developing your *Formula for Success* be consistently conscious of the words you use. Keep your words packed with dramatic vibrancy because you, as a person, are constantly on stage. You're on candid camera and constantly giving a "pitch" or sales talk. You're on the make with the "big sell" every day of your life.

Of course that selling job begins with the baby's first smile and cry. It begins with his first words and continues through a lifetime. Words become public persuasion, agents of charm, the *Impression Circle* that radiates out to everyone around you. So why not use the magic of words? Why not achieve your ends through the language you speak? Why not use your formula?

Make your voice and your pen alive, forceful, pleasant. Give out an air of confidence, strength and character. Whether you are reaching out to one person or to many, speak up to get a response favorable to you. Portray what you have to say. Make your speech comfortably colorful. SELL it! Sell it rhythmically! Sell it by those show-business tricks with change-of-pace, change-of-pitch, volume and quality.

Use the magic of words to achieve your ends. Use them to get other people to do WHAT YOU WANT. Through words build the new you. Build your *Impression Circle*. Build your *Personality Appeal*. Through words influence the world around you. Through words bring about change. Use all the words at your command. Use their power and their glory. Man does not live by bread alone. He feeds on words, so use words to manipulate him. Use words to create the success that will inevitably be yours. Remember that *Forward Thrust* + *Directional Control* = *Goal*. With words indoctrinate yourself with the fact that you CAN be superior. Then prove it!

6

Self-Indoctrination
... Via Words

Why think small and be a
failure? Why be poor? Why
be a failure when it is the rule
of success that if you think
big, and are organized to go
after it, you'll BE big! Why
not use the words that will
get you there? Why not
indoctrinate those words of
success into yourself day
after day?

T here's nothing wrong with admitting you want to be motivated, that you want the Golden Bonuses of life. There's nothing wrong with big wants! The BIG thing to want is to WANT BIG! The big thing to do is to DO BIG! The big thing is to exert mental controls that help you achieve your goals.

In indoctrinating yourself for bigger and better achievements, and using your formula for success, there is no place in your vocabulary for the terminology of self-pity, according to Frank James of Motivational Institute. There's no place for requests for sympathy, no place for fear. Fear carries its own terminology, its own odor. It attracts negatives and more fear.

How To Beat Fear

To neutralize the mind of fear, discouragement and doubt, you have to feed your subconscious mind with words of positive planning, persistence, enthusiasm and faith. You have to indoctrinate yourself with the message of achievement. You have to develop words you can idelibly write as you accomplish goals. You have to dream your little dream and then accomplish it piece by piece.

How to self-indoctrinate yourself

What IS this word indoctrination program? How do you do it? Is there some magic method of induction? How is this mental imagery developed to help create success? Why does imagination play such an important role in pre-planning the pattern of success? How can the success pattern be engraved on your mind? What's the procedure?

From day to day *suggestion* controls us. It is used to help release abilities and talents. It is used to release all the power-potentials of which the brain is capable. By a series of command-control patterns you can indoctrinate anything into your mind, or the minds of others, that you desire. Through self-imposed word patterns you gear yourself to success. With words you step up human physiology, human action, and human thinking. You make people perform to plausible suggestion and it all begins in the mind, YOUR mind.

Without this suggestibility success is not possible. Your mind has to be receptive to it. You have to be able to concentrate attention on an idea and not be distracted. You have to be intelligent enough to receive it.

What IS suggestion?

SUGGESTION is a purposeful and persuasive planting of the success message over and over. You plant it in the subconscious as well as conscious mind and make it grow into the Golden Goals that are yours.

To make your suggestions materialize remain in command of yourself at all times. Be positive! Come right out and say "I will succeed." Then DO it! Believe! Have faith and expectation that your suggestion will come true. Eliminate doubt. Get rid of all words such as "if," "but" or "maybe."

Command without being demanding even as you build the success image in your mind. Reinforce that image with parallel images of you in successful situations. Tune yourself to top performance by setting your mind in the position to achieve it.

Technique One

Do this with words. Do it daily. Do it nightly. Close off your awareness to everything around you and, when you are relaxed, say to yourself the statements which follow.

RULES OF THE ROAD
FOR THE SUCCESSFUL MAN

1. *I know my goals and where I am going.*
2. *To reach these goals I will think first, plan, and THEN act!*
3. *I will do my best to adjust to that which is around me at all times.*
4. *I will look for, and use, new methods to help others as well as myself.*

5. *I will portray charm and maturity at all times.*
6. *My faith and my belief in myself will always be strong.*
7. *I will be confident and competent at all times.*
8. *I will understand my hopes and my prayers, and my aspirations for what they are.*
9. *I will be a leader.*
10. *I will fight for what I want and hold it.*
11. *I will not victimize myself with unproductive emotions.*
12. *I will be kind and courteous to others in the face of adversity.*
13 *I will move into the future with my mind as well as my eyes open.*
14. *I have a solid belief in myself and my capabilities and from this I will not be dissuaded.*

You are indeed the product of your own thinking and the words that you indoctrinate into your mind. You are the product of what happens in those billions of brain cells where lies the trigger to the *"will to act."*

Stimulate this *will to act* with your desires. Hand-feed it! Direct a pipeline of instruction into the channels you would follow and a whole new life will open up for you. Use self-instruction and self-indoctrination as a tool. Use the self-sell and find yourself becoming more competent, more confident, more secure.

Within you is the power to mobilize your abilities, the power to destroy fear, the power to dream and create, the power to convert failure into achievement and turn the products of defeat into victory.

> *Remember this—SUCCESS BEGINS FIRST IN THE MIND. It begins with word-implants and word-indoctrination. It begins with the words with which you buy the future.*

Technique Two

Here's a method used by a financier whom we'll call Tony Kennison because he has requested that he remain anonymous. He gives you four basic steps for using words to indoctrinate yourself for success. As he indicates, "Success, not a person's name, is the thing." Here's Kennison's method of word magic. It's a method of *mind-planting* in which you assume you are already powered to move forcefully into the future. You plant the message of success in your subconscious mind through conscious manipulation, as in *Technique One*. Into the computer of the brain you feed positive action-making data so that you can accomplish your goals.

The Kennison Plan for self-indoctrination

Typewrite the following on a card. Read the forward thrust of these words daily for directional control:

Four Faith And Belief
Steps in Developing Your Forward Thrust
Toward Success

These are

(1) M Y G O A L S (name them)

a. ——————————————NOTE: *Get your goals in focus.*
b. ———————————— *Define them cleanly, sharply,*
c. ———————————— *emphatically. Plan! Know your*
d. ———————————— *objectives. Be motivated with*
e. ———————————— *a strong forward thrust.*

These are
(2) M Y T A L E N T S

a. ——————————————NOTE: *Use your skills and ca-*
b. ———————————— *pabilities advantageously. Es-*
c. ———————————— *tablish your talents. Then train*
d. ———————————— *and use them with intent to*
e. ———————————— *succeed.*

This is how
(3) I W I L L G E T M Y G O A L S

a. ——————————————NOTE: *Choose your route. Be-*
b. ———————————— *come educated and trained in*

c. _____ *your field. Know exactly the way*
d. _____ *to go and be adaptable in case*
e. _____ *of bumps.*

This is my
   (4) T I M E S C H E D U L E

a. _____ NOTE: *Name your target dates.*
b. _____ *Accomplish them one by one*
c. _____ *and feel the exhilarating power*
d. _____ *that flows through you. Tie the*
e. _____ *facts and the goals down with*
                                 words . . . and then with action.

**Develop your subconscious
mind-feeding program**

Just what can you do with the Four Magic Steps of the Kennison Plan for self-indoctrination?

**Here's what the
Kennison Plan accomplishes:**

1. *You establish goals and defined routes*
2. *You develop a time schedule and inventory to accomplish your objectives!*

I prefer to call this method *"Mind-planting."* Kennison calls it *"planned mental programming,"* as he mixes the total ingredients in his personal formula for success so that they jell at once.

Then he does everything he can to make success come true. He provides the fuel for accomplishment, tunes his psychological and physiological motor for high-octane performance and then sets his *Four Steps* to work. In all its living magnificence he primes his subconscious mind, then lets it work out a strong program. Strengthened by faith and belief in himself, Kennison used his program and made a million! So YOU use it! Use it properly and YOU CAN'T FAIL!

How to develop the
tangibles of success

Project the dramatic details of success into YOUR mind! Stage it! Develop it! Produce it! Show it! Out of a program of word-induction into the subconscious mind turn faith and belief into the tangibles of success!

The point is, if you would develop the tangibles of success, you have to know yourself first. Then you have to go after your objectives like Kennison did. You have to use your *forward thrust* knowing that your own brain is a fabulous source of power, a fabulous computer, that you can think faster than you can talk, that you can therefore come up with ideas and words in advance of conversational need, that you can pre-design and determine the program you will use in influencing people to think and act in a particular manner. Realize that *these natural resources are already yours.*

Bess Sondel, in her book, *"Power-Steering with Words"** puts it this way: "We are endowed with a system of controls, physiological as well as psychological, that we use as much in the unconscious as well as the conscious level. The system of controls is built in. The operation of these controls is as natural as life itself."

The point is, if you would achieve success you have to use the controls at your command. You have to use your head and that fabulous center called the "brain." It's the greatest. It's not just an artesian well of words. It contains the mechanism of evaluating and interpreting your career. The brain provides the roadway to success and its power is unlimited! As Dr. Sondel puts it, "To be a self-made man is commendable, but to be a self-making man is glorious."

What developing "concepts"
means to your success

When people obviously become alert to you, you know that you have scored in your *forward thrust*. When you see them move in

---

* Bess Sondel, *Power Steering with Words* (Chicago: Follett Publishing Co., 1964), p. 98.

compliance with your requests you know that your controls are at work. Your line of communication with words is uncut.

To achieve the ends of success you have to develop other factors as well as develop *forward thrust* and *directional control.* Along with the blueprint for goal-getting you have to develop your brain. You have to take advantage of it by developing memory, by developing its operational capacity, by stepping up production of ideas, by mind-planting and mental programming. To this should be added, "Develop your concepts as well."

"Memory," according to psychologist Vince Black, "is stored experience. It is a systematic organization of data by the subconscious mind. This memory creates background upon which to trade in developing the future."

Albert Einstein called these memory-pictures "concepts."* These pictures develop in the storehouse of memory and to experience is added want and motivation. From this picture come you and your goal.

You learn. You think. You interpret. Your wants constantly shape this process and *wants are NOT inherited urgencies!* They are characteristics which have to be acquired.

Behind all words and desires for success are cultivated wants. Behind all ideas and behavior is a formula for the future. If you would use your formula you have to use your head and the memory-pictures and concepts of which it is capable. You have to make use of your desires. You have to need and want and have a purpose for doing.

As you become more and more aware of this process you will more and more be capable of manipulating your mental resources to achieve your goals. You become better capable of decision-making and behavior-control. With greater self-understanding you become better able to use words to control people.

For example, no one goes in "cold" on anything to make a decision! Decisions come only with thinking, with understanding, with capability to make these decisions. In making a decision about achieving success you don't just say, "I will be a success!" You DO something effective to become a success!

Of course you know what you want to do and what you want to be. Of course you want the best things in life. But the best

* Albert Einstein, "Autobiographical Notes," *Library of Living Philosophers,* Vol. III (Chicago: Open Court Publishing Co., 1949), p. 7.

things in life are not free! Your road to tomorrow is replete with necessary decisions. The road is paved with hurts from lack of know-how, with risks, with sacrifices, with losses and with conflict. The consequences are not all golden unless you do that which is necessary to reach those beautiful Golden Goals. Through the magic power of words you can achieve success by manipulating their *forward thrust* and *directional controls*. Exactly how?

Let's take a look at that formula again:

$$FORWARD \ THRUST + DIRECTIONAL \ CONTROL = GOAL$$

Forward thrust is based on what you know. It's based on your imagination, your memory, your concepts, your needs, your wants, your education and training, and your calculated response to it all. It's based on your capacity to decide what you want to do and then DO IT!

Decisions and what they mean to you

Decisions build toward a goal. Good decisions deliberately trim away inefficiency. They help you make better use of your natural resources. They help prevent disaster by choosing a wiser course. They are your range-finder with your goals on target.

Decisions help you move forward. They help you mold the tactics used in *directional control* of people. They help manipulate the guidelines to success so that the program you develop for reaching those goals is coherent.

Put your finger on it— what do you REALLY want?

The time of decision is NOW! What do you *really* want out of life? Name it once more. What is it specifically that you desire? NAME it! How are you going to get there? SAY it! Do you have a purpose? Have you determined or analyzed the route you will go to achieve success in your field? On the line following write your goal. Put your finger on it!

This is my goal: _____

In recapping it all now just how ARE you going to get to that goal? How are you going to manipulate people through the use of words to get to that goal? All right, let's use that dynamo of terminology! Let's use words! Let's communicate!

7

Communication, The Golden Thread Of Success

Success depends on communication! You live or die, in almost every phase of your life, by the necessity to put yourself across. How well you "get through to people" determines the golden thread of that magic cloth called words.

O ne day I sat in on a sales meeting of a major paint manufacturer. Sales manager Rod Duncan had just pulled an old
chestnut out of the hat. He was using it effectively. It was the one
about John Patterson of National Cash in Dayton and the equally
famous Elmer Wheeler. He had three points to make.

Word-Strategy ONE

"Patterson put it this way," said Duncan. 'When you go into a
hat store to sell a cash register talk hats, NOT cash registers!'
Elmer Wheeler said, 'Don't sell the steak—sell the sizzle!' In both
these cases is one pertinent factor—S–E–L–L !

"Selling is communication! Your entire lifetime is one big sell.
It's getting through to people where they live! So use the vitality of
words to get through to them. Use descriptive words that take advantage of fact as well as fancy. Sell words like *'luxury.'* Sell *comfort!* Sell *relaxation* and time for play! Sell *happiness* and *health.*
Sell the satisfaction someone will get from what you have to sell.
Do this and you'll land accounts you previously thought impossible!"

"Particular words are important," he went on to say. "They are
the words people want to hear and our dealers are people. We've
talked about selling our product, but let's talk about selling the
dealer. Let's talk about something near and dear to him. All right,
what does HE want to hear? What's most important?

Word-Strategy TWO

"The most important thing to him is HIM. That's the Big Word:
H–I–M—the real *big* word in successful communication!

"He's not interested in your ideas about anything! He's not
interested in YOUR children or YOUR game of golf. He's not interested in YOUR religion or your political faith. He's interested
in HIS kids, HIS ideas, his hole-in-one on the golf course! So when
you contact him DON'T SELL PAINT! Sell descriptive words!
Most of all sell HIM!

"Ask him—What is YOUR opinion, Mr. Jones? Sell him on
himself by saying, 'The plant is proud of the job you are doing.'
That's hat sales! That's the sizzle from the steak! That's a paint
job . . . a real *snow job* if you do it right.

"Learn to say, *'If you please.'* If he gives you an order, or does something for you, say, *'Thanks.'* Say it so that he hears it! Write him a note so that he remembers it!"

Word-Strategy THREE

"Now, hear this: Never use the word 'I.' Starting as of now delete it from dealer relationships. As far as our dealers are concerned 'I' is the least important word you know.

"Now get out there and sell beauty—NOT paint! Sell HIM—not YOU! Sell the assets that come with both. Use the words that make him see what you are talking about. Use sales aids that help him picture it! Get through to him with words!"

As I sat there in the midst of those sales people the message came through to me loud and clear. I certainly never forgot it. It was a lesson on how to penetrate people. Certainly you have to talk their language. You have to understand them. You have to know how to serenade their egos with communication. You have to use the right words in doing it!

Talk Their Language
And Make That Language Live!

If you would get a point across, make sure that the words you use tell people something they already know! Tell them they will get something they want! But in the telling make sure that what you have to say is understood!

To get people to understand—just that little bit better—speak of things of which they are already well aware. Talk about the tried, the true, the accepted. Remember that people are afraid of anything new. They resent departures from the accepted. They resent being introduced to anything they don't yet understand even when it is something they need. Therefore, to play the right music in public speaking *use their language, their ideas, their ideals, their hopes.* If you are going to get through to them, live at their level of needs and understanding.

For example, Kelly Fuerhman simply lost contact with people

because of his way of life. Kelly was a scientist. He lived in vitro. His was a test-tube world and he talked biophysics, ate it and slept with it.

One day his company sent him out to speak to a Rotarian noontide club. The meal was great but Kelly was a dud. As a luncheon speaker he fell on his face because his jargon was way out. No one understood. Instead of coming down to lay level and connecting the story of his experiments with what they already understood and knew, or hooking his point to something they wanted like longer life, he spent 20 minutes that would have been a stunner for biophysicists but left the Rotarians wishing they hadn't come. On the way out of the hotel one of the boys was heard to remark: "You sure this Fuerhman's not from Mars? He doesn't speak our language at all!"

Sell what they want!
Say what they want to hear
And be a wanted man!

Michael Koehl got his job selling beauty supplies. The majority of his contacts were women. At first his calls were straight-on with no finesse. To them he was "just another salesman" until he came up with the procedure that made him a *"wanted man."*

What did this jolly little man with the Santa Claus figure do? He simply became more compatible to the beauty needs of women and their rituals for becoming lovely.

The moment he became conscious of *THEIR needs* he started to sell. *He educated them in THEIR LANGUAGE.* He studied his products before he presented them as that answer to their needs. He went to conventions and picked up sales tricks. He studied competitive products. He became a walking encyclopedia on the lore of cosmetics through the ages. At the manufacturer's plant he learned ingredients and their purposes and how to apply them. He went to New York and Chicago for further professional advice.

The moment he became conscious of the cosmetics story his visits to the "girls" became a seminar.

Mike walked in and the operators clustered eagerly around him despite the head operator's admonition to "Get back to work!"

What did Mike do? He demonstrated the advantages of beauty aids. He gave practical training. He gave them understanding. He showed them how the products would improve personal beauty. He added a little humor to make them laugh and even the gags were tied into the product. While his customers were all breathlessly wrapped up in his smooth pitch he made his appeal for action.

Sales jumped! Each week Mike presented a different item. It was nothing new, just the regular line, and it wasn't without cost to Koehl. He spent weeks in research. He built up his own understanding and know-how. But when he presented a product-demonstration he sounded like he knew what he was talking about. *He talked their language* while publicly speaking. He used the right words and talked himself not only into popularity as a cosmetics salesman but into the state distributorship as well. The last time I talked to Mike his net take was $38,000 a year.

Don't just talk their language— give something free

No one accepts anything you say unless what they hear and see makes them believe it. They *have* *t*o be convinced! They have to be manipulated into action and this is where Mike Koehl clicked. Of course he used salesmanship! Of course he used showmanship! Why not?

"Girls," he'd say, "this isn't just another beauty product! It's something that *you* can use! You want a lovely skin, don't you? All right, I want you to use this product on yourself. Use it for one week! Free! Go ahead! Apply it to your elbows. Note the soft gentle texture that follows. Now try it on your hands. If it does this to your hands and elbows, think of what it will do for your face. Wipe. . . . Now note how the skin takes on the characteristics of youth. How many women do you know who want to look young again? All of them! So help them! Help them help themselves to yesterday. Help a few and the message will spread so fast you won't be able to handle the volume of business!"

The Value Of Words

People remember only a tenth of what you say. As a result you have to overdress everything said to make that tiny percentage click.

Success depends on getting through to people

Any success with words is directly proportional to your ability to penetrate the public mind. It is dependant on the ease with which you gain access to people and get them to believe what you have to say.

Some minds are open. Some minds are closed. Some are easy to penetrate and are replete with understanding. Others are blankly impervious, negative, and callously closed to the traffic of human relationships. To demonstrate roughly the kinds of minds with which you will have to cope, in achieving success through the use of words, I submit the following categories. Here's an inside tip: *in listening to conversations there are three ways to classify the minds of people.* Note that (1) GREAT MINDS discuss ideas; (2) AVERAGE MINDS discuss events; (3) SMALL MINDS discuss people. All of such minds I refer to roughly as *roadways.* I do this because minds are the routes through to the people who possess them. Such roadways are: (1) The *Freeway Mind;* (2) The *Toll-Road Mind;* (3) The *Roadblock* or *Detour Mind,* and, (4), The *Dead-End Mind.*

Here's the explanation:

THE KINDS OF MINDS
WHICH YOU MUST STIMULATE

1. *The freeway mind*

   Here are the glories to the open road of success. The open mind receives your ideas with full acceptance. It's a bright mind, an alert mind that is unbiased in its belief of you and your ideas. It's a throughway to acceptance and the type of mind you wish everyone had.

2. *The toll-road mind*

   This is the mind where you pay the toll of winning their confidence by payment of friendliness. Once you are through the courting stage of words and get through to them, the freeway to your objectives is non-stop.

3. *The roadblock or detour mind*

This mind pretends to understand. This person pretends to listen but he doesn't hear you. You can see that the highway is clear on the other side of the barrier, but you can't get through.

4. *The dead-end mind*

This is the mind of a person who is against you from the start. As far as he is concerned you might just as well shut up. You're against a blank wall because he isn't interested and he doesn't care about you or about anything you have to say.

Naturally you want a successful relationship with people. You want their love, their belief, their respect, their cooperation. You want happiness.

Then how do you get on the Freeway? How do you convert the Dead-Enders and get through to them? When you get through to them, what do you have? You have success through words and here's how to do it.

**How to open up the
other person's mind**

*The quickest way to get through the mental roadblocks
of people is to get their acceptance!*

*Here's how to
do it with words:*

1. *Agree with people*

Let them know they're right. Listen to their problems. Let them know you care. Open their minds through understanding. Agree with them and stop an argument before it starts. See the problem from the other person's point of view and you will open up your own mind as well as theirs.

2. *Get rid of that "holier-than-thou" attitude*

We are all much superior to the dead-end mind of "the other guy." Whether you like to think it or not, it's true that everyone has a secret yen to see someone else fail, to see them hurt. Such people get a kick out of gossip because it makes them feel superior by hurting the other person. Through gossip such a person becomes the wonderful one and the other person very terrible. We gloat over failure. We run down or minimize the accomplishments of others and in so doing hurt our own chances for success. The answer, then, to this holier-than-thou attitude is to HELP THE OTHER FELLOW WHETHER HE IS RIGHT OR WRONG and you'll "get through to him" faster than you think. By being on his side, you are already "in."

Holier-than-thou
statements to avoid:
1. "With a voice like that she should be a foghorn."

2. "They took him off the vice squad and put him in the Traffic Division as helicopter observer. He's had his nose in the air ever since."

Open up the minds of other people so that they will be more receptive to suggestion. Get them tactfully into position for persuasion and remember that *tact many times is nothing more than the ability to shut your own mouth before someone else wants to!*

3. *Persuade, but never pressure, others*

Have the patience to help people. Help them to their objectives but don't press them! Help them *see* their objectives just a little bit more clearly. The moment their minds open up you simply walk in. Give them support when they are in difficulty and you will have won friends through persuasion. Help them see what's right for them and remember that *the successful person sees what's right with the world. HE DOES NOT SEE WHAT'S WRONG!* If you would know and understand people, listen closely to conversation. Once you understand them, move in, but no pressure!

4. *Get rid of pet hates, grudges, and that "superior air"*

The quickest way to use the right words to get rid of the other person's hates and grudges is to say: "You're right. I'm wrong." Remember that *hates are defensive, diversionary tactics used to prove superiority over someone else.* Using such tactics at no time wins friends and influences people. Hates grow out of fear, inferiority and foolishness. Hate is the inability to admit you're wrong. It's the pighead refusal to make amends, the dead-end of minds. It is blindness, paralysis and masquerade. It is the inability to express the commission of a mistake when all it would take to change everything is those four magic words: "You're right. I'm wrong!" Be the first to say it and forget your pride. Be the first to do so whether you are right or not. Be the first to say, "I like you," and see the difference it makes. Try going out of your way to demonstrate that you are not half so superior as you have pretended in the past.

5. *Admit you're not perfect*

Stop acting like you're always right and others are imperfect, that you have no weaknesses of your own. Admit that you too have problems and take the other person off guard. When you indicate that you too are human and fallible they will appreciate you even more.

6. *Stop griping and start getting somewhere*
Some matters are simply beyond control. Some mat-

ters may be directly under the control of others. Some
we can handle ourselves if the problem is brought to
our attention. Often we fail to take advantage of what
is in front of us because we have not recognized opportunity. We haven't taken advantage of luck and
*luck is what happens when preparation meets oppor-
tunity.* As Charles F. Kettering once said: "You never
stub your toe standing still. The faster you go, the
more chance there is of stubbing your toe, but the
more chance you have of getting somewhere."

It was that way with a junior executive I know. He came in complaining that there was no place to go in his company. Two of the
boss's sons would prevent possible executive promotion. Even the
board of directors was composed of relatives. It was a family
operation.

"I know I'm wrong in griping, but what can I do?" he wanted
to know.

"Do you really want to stay with the company?" I asked.

"Yes."

"Does your boss have a daughter?"

"Yes."

"Is she pretty?"

"Gorgeous."

"Does she like you?"

"She invites me over quite often."

"Is she of marriageable age?"

Tom looked at me curiously. His eyes widened. A big grin
broke. "So *that's* the way to do it! All it takes is the magic words
and I become part of the family. I get where I want to go in the
company! Thanks, Doc. That sure is a shot in the arm."

You do best what
you like to do

Most people fail at jobs that go unrewarded and at jobs in which
they have been inadequately placed. Success never occurs to those
who are unhappy in what they are doing. *The highest reward for
your work is not what you get for it but what you become because*

of it. An old tour guide once said, "The road to success is dotted with a lot of tempting parking places." So avoid too many rest stations. Travel light and straight on as you do what you like to do.

Use The Golden Thread
Of Communication Daily

From the Fifteenth Chapter of Proverbs of Solomon comes the statement, "The tongue of the wise useth knowledge aright: but the mouth of fools poureth out foolishness."

Of all the millions of copyrighted inventions no one as yet has created a brake for the tongue and an accelerator for the brain. After all is said and done, more is said than done and success doesn't come this way. When the tongue is overused the mouths of fools poureth out foolishness indeed.

Communicate! Get through to people where they live! Use the vitality of words: descriptive words that take advantage of fact and truth, words that sell what people want to buy, words like *health, luxury, comfort.* Sell them the satisfactions that come with personal possession. Use the magic words that touch their pride and weave this golden thread through their lives daily.

Use effective talk, as did Andrew Carnegie throughout his lifetime. When he was a boy in Scotland he had a litter of rabbits but no food. As a result he "promoted" the neighborhood boys. He told them he would name a rabbit after each if every day they would pick clover and dandelions. The plan worked. The rabbits waxed fat. Years later Carnegie tried the same gimmick. He used the same line, the golden energy of communication, the same psychology. He built a tremendous steel plant in Pittsburgh and named it after the president of the Pennsylvania Railroad. He called it the J. Edgar Thompson Steel Works and Mr. Thompson was delighted. It didn't take too much to sell him on buying rails from the company that bore his name—and this is the art of using words advantageously. As sales manager Rod Duncan said: "The most important word to him is HIM. That's the BIG word. That's successful communication." That's the way to use communication as you develop the golden thread of success. That's the staff to lean on.

8

Words, Not Bread, Are The Staff Of Life

If you are still fighting to get up at the top YOU *HAVE NOT YET DEVELOPED THE RIGHT WORDS OR ACTIONS.* You have not yet tooled up for success. Through words you have not yet gotten through to people with that magnetic power that draws people into your zone of influence. As yet you have not come up with expressions that work social or commercial magic.

Dollars are the blood of trade? Money talks? Who said? Let's kick that around a bit and consider something more basic than dollars. Let's say instead that words and know-how, rather than money, are the blood of trade. Let's develop the concept that *words and know-how in business are the staff of life!*

Through words, business and industry, professions and social circles move to new areas of achievement, new products, new research, new outlets. Through words they diversify.

Let's go another step forward now with the phenomenon of words. Let's say that if you ARE a success you can't rest on your oars in today's market. No industry that produces one or more winning products can afford to relax.

It has to keep coming up with winners and bright new words and pictures to describe them. Now add another paradox. Once you market a winner you have to come right back and dissatisfy a previously satisfied customer. He has to be made to want next year's "new model" and this new model craze has to be kept constantly awake. Most manufacturers today force this stimulus by engineering the quality of products to last two years. It's systematic sabotage which is covered with the glory of words.

To make the market more susceptible to all this, to "soften up the market," the "manipulators of the public mind," the advertising agencies, place the public mind in the juicer-and-squeezer of public relations, propaganda, publicity, promotion and merchandising machine. Desire is teased with glamorous words and pictures. Millions of dollars are poured into words that pre-test the market before more millions go into experimental models and even more multi-millions into the advertising that follows.

Fascinating new desirables are publicized and portrayed. Imagination is stimulated to develop new wants. The product becomes irresistible. As a result people become dissatisfied with what they have. They no longer want their "old" home, their "old" car, their "old" refrigerator, their "old" cigarette. They want that which is new. It has to be fresh. It has to supply their newly indoctrinated *need* and newly developed *want* and this is exactly what words do. Words, in this manner become the lifeblood of industry. Words, rather than dollars, are the staff of life. The business that does not advertise goes broke in the face of competition. Without the right words and actions at the right time there is no lifeline. Proof of the pudding is in the thousands of small businesses that go broke each year because they never learned that the staff of life is not dollars but words which make those dollars pay off. Therefore, by such a process of deduction, we determine that without words there is no money. Without money there is no bread. Therefore, BREAD IS NOT THE STAFF OF LIFE! MONEY IS NOT THE STAFF OF LIFE! It's the original words you need to get both.

The same evolution of words
applies to careers

In your reach for personal success you go through much the same evolution as does industry. You develop the product of your own speciality. You polish and shine it. You jazz it up with an attractive chrome trim. You make it so tempting that *someone* has to have it. It may be your sales ability; it may be the architectural drawings you create. It may be your beautiful face and figure. It may be the quality of your voice that makes you a top singing star.

Whatever it is, that *someone* has to have your services, your product, your brains, your beauty. Industry, for example, has to have YOU and what you can do with words and pictures because it cannot survive without the likes of you to operate its business.

Without you, industry cannot bring dollars into its coffers. Therefore, you are their pitchman from the moment you are born. Their sell begins with your first bawling cry and come-on smile as a baby. It's a lifetime of salesmanship that begins when you first begin to talk. From there on in you keep priming the pump of yours and other people's needs.

It is YOU who create the glorious achievements of industry and business. Because of this *they need you!* They *want* you! You know this and because of this you keep building the attractiveness that is you. You use industry's own techniques in creating a bright product. You publicize your personal product and put youself in the marketplace. You use big business' own techniques for creating a model that someone else desires. You create a need for your services and you do it through words, know-how, and action. As a result you attract higher and higher salaries and fringe benefits.

Words and know-how are the attractions that create the magnetic pull for dollars. They are the staff of your economic life and to this there is no alternative.

Kick the theme around further, if you like, but it keeps coming out the same: *Words, not bread, are the staff of life as well as the staff of your success.* . . . How these words are all directly related to people, and in turn to success, is noted in the tender areas of human relationship.

Ten Vital Needs
In Your Approach To People

In developing an awareness of people, and achieving success because of your ability to get through to them with words, there is a necessity to be tuned to the following ten factors: (1) *creating an impression* with the right approach, (2) *developing personality appeal* for getting through to people, (3) *developing key phrases* to which others may attach themselves, (4) *expressing your gratitude*, (5) *avoiding hurting someone's feelings*, (6) *forgiving and forgetting*, (7) *using praise* where it counts, (8) *avoiding criticism of others*, (9) *using name-calling successfully*, (10) *finding something good to say about everyone* no matter what their problem.

Each of these factors sounds like a trifle, yet each is a world-beater. Each factor learned and used gives you a kind of rapport with people that involves them in helping you achieve success. Each is a kind of magic door to *directional control* over people. Each proves over and over that words, not bread, are the staff of the successful life at any strata of living. Each is a dynamic force in developing your personal power-urge. Each is brilliantly keyed to fortune and fame.

Prevent wrong impressions through
your "approach" to people

Approach is the terminology of sales people referring to the direct route to making money.

The approach to people is action enforced by words.
It is motion accompanied by the dramatics of kindness,
courtesy and being gracious through words.

How well you make this approach, how well you dramatize it and convert it into an effective vehicle for selling a product, or your personality, is determined by what you put into it. It also determines what you get out.

If you are a salesman, how many times have you lost a sale because your approach was wrong? What was missing? What was too much or too little? Were you courteous? Were you gracious? Did you have the right touch? Did you please the other person? Were the words and the music right?

A discount house makes a fortune through "approach"

Tom Malone of Furniture Mart Industries demonstrated how he trains his sales personnel on "approach." We walked into one of his Midwest chain-operated outlets. Each store was a giant "barn" packed from front to back with merchandise ranging from cheapies to prestige imports from Europe. Style varied from slim Danish moderns to the heavy brawn of the Italian Renaissance. Furniture for the flat-pocketbook crowd and furniture for the well-heeled. All of it available at discount prices.

Malone explained: "With each customer we take it free and easy. No tension. No prestige. No push. We approach quietly, politely, attentively. We open up with the time of day—'Good morning,' 'Good afternoon,' or 'Good evening.' Then, simply, courteously, quietly we add, 'May I help you?' or, 'Is there something I can do for you, sir?'

"Meanwhile, the customer is sizing you up. He's eyeballing you for a quick run-down on your clothing, your stature, carriage, odor, and habits. He's already fixed an opinion of the store by looking at the sales person. On the other hand you may look right but you can destroy the store's image by using the destructive negatives that kill a sale before it starts.

"Remember this—the customer did us a favor by coming in the store!"

"Take it from me," said Malone emphatically, "there are particular things NOT to say. Here are some of them. Never open up on a customer with—'You got trouble?' 'You want something?' 'What is it?' 'Want to be waited on?' 'Something on your mind?'

"Phrases like this are murder. They ruin the store's image. They develop wrong impressions and they're costly even in a discount house."

Malone says that a good *approach* leaves good memories. A bad approach destroys it. As he puts it, "I could spend five grand a week in newspaper and TV advertising to lure prospects into my stores, but if my employees turn away people with the wrong approach I might just as well never have invested the money!"

Malone has proved his point by developing a big business. By pioneering discount houses he helped revolutionize sales trends. How he indoctrinates his sales staff has made him his fortune. He made it *big* based on "the approach" and follow-through . . . all in words.

Now add Malone's *TWELVE-POINT PROGRAM* for using words to make the sales approach stick and maintain the proper image. It's his "tough line" but he's made millions with it. Maybe you can too. Here now, in esssence, is what I recorded from his sales staff meetings: —

TWELVE-POINT PROGRAM FOR
USING WORD-POWER
TO MAKE THE CUSTOMER SINCERELY YOURS

1. *Get them thinking positively!*

"You've wrapped your client up the moment he starts nodding yes to easily answered questions. Set the stage for this. Eliminate all negatives. Keep him saying yes. Keep him off balance with your pitch until you're ready to close the deal.

"How can you make people receptive to you? How can you make them more pervious?

"You do it by saying things that are agreeable to them. You talk in terms that create no back-talk, no resistance. You talk the language lay people understand. You develop similar goals and agree on the same matters. Once you get a prospect saying yes to that on which you already agree you can suck him into the sales trap. He will be placed in a position where he can't retreat. He can't withdraw because he's already committed. With this in mind keep your sales pitch positive. Permit no negatives to enter the picture at any time. Keep that person saying 'Yes' by punching across the positives at all times!"

2. *Know what's in the other person's mind*

"Hear him out. Give him ample time to talk. Learn by listening and watching. When you see the opportunity step in for that all important signature on the dotted line. The only alternative is CASH!"

3. *Understand the other person's prejudices*

4. *Watch for preconceived ideas*

5. *Wait for hot emotions* (yours, theirs) *to cool off*

6. *Agree with them*

"What does it cost to disagree? Everything! The moment you lose tempo with the other person you're dead. So's your product. You have lost a friend and killed your own possibilities for success. By the wrong use of words you lose all of us money!"

7. *Appeal to the emotions of others*

"People act in accordance with what they feel and too seldom with what they think. The person who would be a success cannot afford this. Emotions must play no role in his decisions or acts. His reasoning has to control him at all times.

8. *Know how the other person feels*

"In selling and dealing with people you deal with them through their senses and sensitivities. *You deal with people through THEIR eyes . . . not through yours!* You deal with them through *THEIR emotions*. Not yours! So understand their prejudices. Understand their hurts, their hates, their grudges and suspicions.

Understand their fears. Most of all *understand their wants!*"

9. *Demonstrate sympathy, kindness and understanding*

"Even in the most frustrating moments, be kindly. Later, in privacy you can beat hell out of a punching bag or kick a garbage can in the alley, or run a lonesome mile to get rid of your tension."

10. *Admit when you're wrong*

"There's no faster way to get through to people than the frank admission that you've made a booboo. Be frank! Be honest! Say you were wrong, or in error, BUT DON'T APOLOGIZE! Such an open admission steps you up in the other person's eyes. If our furniture proves to have a flaw, we take it back promptly. No questions asked. The customer may be dead wrong but for money's sake he's always right!"

11. *Be diplomatically lavish with compliments*

"Compliments are meaningless to those who have often achieved. They are empty phrases unless they touch on something intimately personal. For example, Jack Thompson, division manager of Crile Motors is a champion golfer. Time after time people have congratulated him on his consistent wins and he doesn't hear them. The moment you talk about his blue ribbon setters his ears perk up. His dogs are his pride and his joy. His golf is a method for publicizing his car business. So to touch Thompson on a sensitive spot you touch his pride and his joy . . . his dogs."

12. *Get people to make decisions*

"A sale is never a sale until it's closed! It's never consumated until a decision is made. Because of this you have to develop the words that make people feel they have made the right choice, that that which they have chosen is first grade. Remove all doubts. Eliminate their fears. Make them feel secure. Wipe out all possible phases of indecision.

"How do you handle it with words? Create a want. Make them hungry for the item. Develop the picture of product-desirability. Spur their imagination and forget the details. With words, as persuaders and manipulators, stimulate the client's desire. To help him make a decision talk practically. Talk color, seductive sculptured lines. What you DON'T talk about is price! Spur their desires first! Flatter them! Say—'With all these plus factors you'd expect the price to be higher, wouldn't you? But it's not! It's only $———!' "

The music of success
has sales pitch

As Malone says, there's a time when every successful salesman, lecturer, statesman, or even author becomes increasingly aware that he is developing a "smooth line." He's more and more able to set the right lyrics to the music of success. He finds himself growing more adept at turning it on and off at will. It's his "sales pitch" and it flows to fit his needs and the circumstances of the moment.

In directing this symphony of success it is wise to note that the sales pitch you use on one person will not work on another. The lecturer who has a hot angle going for him in Hoboken drops dead in Santa Fé with the same routine. A joke I used successfully in Dayton, Ohio, laid a bomb during a lecture in the ballroom of New York's Waldorf-Astoria.

At first you don't know why this happens. Then you begin to inventory what you've said. If you are observant and understanding you make some findings that are startling. Your findings will be on the effect of words on the audience upon whom you use them. From these findings come ideas and "angles" that are good universally, and are acceptable almost anywhere. All you have to do is adapt them to time, place and occasion.

How do you determine which of the little gems are most effective? Personally I use a pocket-sized tape recorder. This high sensitivity instrument picks up all background response to my lectures. Laughter, applause, dissent, all are included. By experience then I find phrases, ideas, that are striking a common note. When this happens I make note of them, reuse them, polish them, couch the same ideas in different colors and flavors and adapt them to other areas of conquest.

Through consistent study of an approach to people you soon determine where you are clicking and where you are falling flat on your face. You quickly learn the words to use and the words to drop. By self-study you make your own opportunities. Through product-control (your speech products) you develop the personalized selling phrases that makes for successful presentation and even more successful word-vending.

Start today on the development of YOUR selling phrases. Notice what affects people. Notice how you can touch these heart strings with nothing more than words, words that can be as gentle as down or as explosive as an atomic warhead. Notice how you begin to fit tried and true "key phrases" into each new circumstance. Notice how easily you adapt and sway with your audience. Notice how simple the power of words begins to come to you as you influence people day after day.

How to parlay the pretense
of being an oaf

There's a time when appearing stupid is an asset. Such a time is when you appear ignorant about a matter in which you may be a specialist but you don't let the other fellow know it. Let him explain. Let him take the spotlight. There's nothing more important to him than HIM, so let him talk. Let him appear to be the authority and listen as if you were attending opening night of a new world. Listen intently. Laugh at his jokes. Render sympathy if that's what he needs. Parlay the words of the affable oaf into the fancy payoff of friendship. Sure it's a cornball approach, but it works on many who would otherwise be impervious to your approach.

Gratitude And Its Role
In Every "Big" Man's Life

Stop and think about it. How many times have your friends gone to bat for you? How often have they gone out of their way? Think of their many little kindnesses, unselfish acts, delightful surprises, sharing when there was too little to share, the flower on your desk, the birthday card, doing for you when ill, waiting for you when you were long overdue, doing monotonous jobs with never a whimper, giving you a shoulder to cry upon, moral support to brace you, a smile that says you still have love and friends.

These are the people to whom you should express your gratitude in developing words as your staff of life.

Gratitude is something
graciously warm and friendly

Gratitude is the feeling you have for someone who has done something good. It's a desire to repay a favor, a thankfulness for a good turn. Gratitude is the act of showing appreciation for kindness, big or small, so that others are made to know it in return. Express it because when you look at yesterday without regret, and look at tomorrow without fear, you're on your way to being a success. You are destined to be exactly what you want to be!

WHAT YOU CAN DO
TO SHOW GRATITUDE

1. *No matter how small the service someone does for you, acknowledge it.* Do it immediately. Put it in the precise words of pleasure.

2. *Smile! It costs nothing.* A smile is your personal signature to a statement of thanks and everyone welcomes it.

3. *Promptly say "Thank you"* for every service rendered, or any favor done.

4. *Look for places, people and opportunities to express your thanks.*

5. *Make others feel welcome.* Voice your welcome to everyone!

6. *Give encouragement,* whenever and wherever you can.

7. *Reach out your hand* when others need your strength. Say that you understand.

8. *Give yourself each day* in every way and what you say and do will give someone the courage to go on.

There's certainly a place for gratitude in every man's life and this is especially true of those who seek success.

There's No Room For Modesty In The Pyramid Climb

In the reach for success, and in success itself, there is little or no room for modesty. There's even less room for pretense of modesty. Let's take that idea from the top.

Success puts you in a goldfish bowl and life in the spotlight makes you subject to constant observation, applause and continued promotion. So let your light shine forth. Don't be modest! When you click at something, step front-line center for applause!

"Hurt Feelings" And The Problems They Cause In Success

As you move up out of mediocrity, remember that there is no place for "hurt feelings" or any of the vocal expressions that indicate it. Like modesty, there is certainly no place for punctured emotions in those who would be successful.

Energy-loss from hurt feelings is great

Toxic waste floods the body when feelings are hurt. The bitterness of emotion rides the blood stream. Real or fancied humiliation and hurt converts the human body into a receptacle for defeat. Indigestion starts. The individual is extremely tired. He can't sleep. His heart is affected. Stomach ulcers begin.

Hurt feelings and anger may make a person drive his car "like crazy." Factory men on the boring mills may ruin thousands of dollars worth of steel because they are "mad at the boss." Lack of understanding, hostility and hate indicate that someone has for-gotten, or didn't have, the right choice of words. Someone did not use thoughtful diplomacy.

In other words, hurt feelings play an influential role.

BAND-AIDS FOR
"HURT FEELINGS"

1. *KNOW why and when feelings get hurt*

   It is more than likely that the reason for someone's hurt feelings lies within some weakness of your own.

2. *Hold out your hand in friendship*

   NEVER ever turn your back on those who need you. *Tell* them you like them, that you want to help them. Then DO it!

3. *Lower the walls you've built around yourself*

   No one can enter a world that is closed against him. Open the door. Smile. Invite people into your life. Tell them you care.

4. *Develop enthusiasm about everything*

   Even at the cost of appearing to bubble, be efferves-cent with words. Spread compliments. Let a smile be your umbrella on every rainy day. Use the tested clichés that make people think you're great.

5. *Empty your mind of real or fancied wrongs*

   Why get upset and let the wrong words pour out? Why tear your soul apart for something that doesn't amount to a hill of beans and then say something that you will always regret. Never argue. Reason goes out the window when anger walks in. No arguments, no mat-ter how sound, are anything other than sound. Argu-ments, and speaking without thinking to hurt someone's feelings, are just like shooting without taking aim.

6. *Do unto others with no thought of thanks*

7. *Bestow love and you'll get it back in return*

Cast the bread of words upon the waters of love and it will come back cake.

8. *You are free to do and say as you please only when you please others*

9. *Never gossip!*

Beware of half-truths. The part you hear may be the wrong half. Gossip is something negative that someone has developed and then enlarged. As a friend of mine says, "Gossip is the making of a mountain out of molehill by piling up dirt." She says that "gossip travels fastest over the sour-grapevine and the person who imbibes of it suffers from acute indiscretion." To prevent a gossiping tongue, prevent gossiping ears. Close your ears to gossip and walk away! Remember there's nothing wrong with having nothing to say. Just don't say it out loud. A gossip talks about others. A bore talks about himself. The successful person always talks about YOU . . . TO YOU.

10. *Be kind*

Kindness is something which you just can't possibly give away. You can bestow it in words and act but you will find it keeps coming right back. Emerson said the sweetest music is not in oratorios but in kind words, so use them! Use them every day of your life, as your staff of life, and you will cause no one's feelings to be hurt.

11. *Forgive, forget, and SAY so!*

Arnold H. Lowe, Minneapolis clergyman, says: "Where there is continuous harping on any mistake, or any misdeed, there is no forgiveness. Forgiveness is a conclusive act. Nagging is a continued irritation. It is a disease. We must cure it, for it breeds another's rebellion and lays the foundation of antagonism and resentment."

12. *Laugh at yourself*

Nothing is more useful than the ability to laugh at your own defects. Lincoln made fun of his homeliness. During a debate Douglass accused Lincoln of being two-faced. Without hesitation the rail-splitter responded: "I leave that to my audience. If I had two faces would I be wearing *this* one?"

Praise! Praise! Praise!

If you would enjoy being liked by others, feed them on praise. No matter what the circumstance, big or little, always diplomatically praise. Do it privately. Do it publicly. Do it directly or by methods that are strategically indirect. When the other fellow wins, gets a promotion, or has a small current success, go up, stick out your hand in congratulations and give him praise. No matter how you feel about the whole thing, PRAISE HIM! Let's take some examples of how this works:

EXAMPLES:

1. *Fran Dicksone* was an outstanding sportswoman. Her tremendous tennis serve took her to the international matches in England. She played hard but, win or lose, she always praised her opponents. She was the first to run around the net and hug them tight. This not only pleased her opponents but gave Fran a superior edge. She *looked* big by saying nice things. By showing them more than cute lace panties she won popularity and fame.

2. *Mel Francis* saw his working partners moved up to executive positions in his company before he knew that HE was the one who was being tested. Each time Mel swallowed his hurt as his friends moved up. He pocketed his pride and rammed down the pounding surge of selfish envy and jealousy that is normal to everyone. He congratulated the men who were advanced. Openly, sincerely, and honestly he demonstrated praise. He walked right up and shook hands and

said warmly: "Congratulations, Johnny. It couldn't have happened to a nicer guy!" But Mel Francis, the truly nice guy, is the one who today is president of of his company. Those whom he congratulated earlier are those who now give him their staunchest support.

Render words of praise freely

Never ask for credit for something done. Don't expect it! But do give it readily! Let others think they are in control even as you manipulate them into a position where you are the true master. Tell them: "You've done a great job. You sold more merchandise than the other sales people and the company is proud of you. Here are your tickets for a week in the sun at Nassau."

Praise and encouragement create good end-results. Uncomplimentary remarks, criticism, disparagement, even silence, can detroy. Therefore use words of praise, and remember:

The praise-phase always pays!

Criticism

Criticism is a cutting edge. No one likes it including you and none of the words in your vocabulary should ever be formed to fit such a pattern.

Four reasons why criticism occurs

When criticism occurs
it indicates:

1. Inadequate social training
2. Low mentality level
3. Emotional stress
4. Being frustrated due to dealing with circumstances beyond control.

No matter what causes the initial trouble, use discretion in handling any situation. Be humane where humans are concerned.

Be understanding. Show compassion. Use the following suggested word-and-action techniques as an approach to getting people to like you.

How to Prevent Criticism

1. *Provide no opportunity for adverse circumstances to jockey you into position to cause you, or to cause others, hurt*

   If the other person is well versed in his occupation, for example, there is no need to castigate him for an errror. Merely eliminate the problem that brought about conflict in the first place.

2. *Shoulder some of the impact*

   You can still get your point across even while shouldering part of the blow. When one of your personnel makes an error, here are some suggested words to handle the problem: "The same thing could have happened to me, Miss Jones. But next time let's do it this way."

3. *Dull the edge of all social blows*

   How do you do it with words?

   Example:

   > Say to her, "You're doing this job nicely, Miss Jones. You are going to be a valuable part of our team. To help you a little more here's a suggestion to facilitate your job."

   In other words let her know you care. *Always praise people before doing a repair job on an error.* Never criticize or bluntly censor anyone!

4. *Come right out and ask if there are any questions or dissatisfactions*

5. *Show appreciation—give awards*

   Nothing steps up performance better than the giving of an award. We are all tuned to the award system.

The top of the pyramid is the point toward which we climb. Fringe benefits along the way are rungs that help those rugged upward steps and no man can get to the top of the success ladder with his hands in his pockets. He also needs his hands free to accept awards for jobs well done. By showing appreciation you help guarantee his improved performance in the future.

6. *Never hire people incapable of the job you expect to be done!*

The Beautiful Act
Of "Name-Calling"

Calling another person by his given name is *strategy!* No one in the world is more important to the other person than himself. To be called by name is music unto his ears. Personalized attention is the sweetest music this side of heaven and you can have this angelic orchestration by playing on the melody of names.

The art of "name-calling" is not in the remembering but in *the powerful diplomacy of focused attention.* The person's name, as a spotlighted word, brings attention to him. Pronouncing his name properly multiplies his pleasure in hearing it. Being able to spell it, as well as say it, indicates you care, that you have remembered, that you have learned the art of getting through to people by utilizing that pleasurable link called "name-calling," that you have the ability to galvanize attention with a word—HIS name—his name which is the most pleasurable sound known to man. The beautiful act of name-calling isn't just diplomacy. In the magic hustle of words, it's a way of handling people if you would be a success.

Never ask, "How are you?"

Asking about a person's health is for doctors only! Let it lie there rather than get an organ recital. Why request the torrent of negatives? Ask a businessman, "How's business?" and everything comes out black. The majority are negative. When people are well, or doing well, they will seldom admit it; so I repeat, never say "How are you?" never say, "How's business?"

Instead, say, "You're looking great!" . . . "Your business has certainly taken on a new look!"

Offer praise. Be complimentary. Make the recipient receptive to you through praise. Work inside his shell. People *want to believe praise,* so *give* them praise! They need that "lift" so vital to their egos. What have you got to lose? What people don't need is to be reminded of their problems. Instead pick out something nice to say. Compliment a woman on her new dress, her lovely jewelry, her coiffure. Give her the big build-up. The ego lift you give her (or anyone else) makes her "feel good." The point is that when you have something to say, say something nice. Be respectful. Be loving. Be kind. Be without resentment. Employ finesse and diplomacy if you would win friends and influence people. Say nothing if you have nothing to say.

If you would use words as your vehicle to success use words of goodness, words of happiness and praise. Use words that help you step up the executive ladder with your hands out of your pockets and on the rungs. If you would live and serve in today's world remember that *words, not bread, are the staff of life!* Clichés? You're right! They are! They are clichés by which people live, so use them! See how beautifully they work day after day!

Words—
The Motivators
That Rule Your Life

Words are NOT something
under glass with a sign above
inscribed, "Don't touch."
They are vital, living things
when seen or heard. Packed
with associations, inflections,
and innuendo, they pass from
mind to mind in a powerful
exchange of meaning. As
instruments of human
motivation, words are
dynamic factors that
dominate and rule your life!

H ow do you get through to people? You get through to people
by getting at the things that motivate them. If it's their pride,
you stimulate their pride. If its their vanity, you give their vanity
a public relations *snow job*. Let's face it—100 per cent of all people
are susceptible to the hypnosis of words, 95 per cent of them can be
motivated, 75 per cent of them can be channeled into predictable
responses through the use of phrases and slogans. Through WORDS
you invade their lives. You get through to their feelings, their
ideas, their heart strings, and manipulate them to the tune you
would play.

The name of the game
is "They want"

In human motivation you play *"They want."* You learn what they
want. Then you help them get it. You talk them into feeling important. You tell them that they are worthy, that they can be trusted,
that within them are the elements of greatness, that they can achieve
their goals. It's a *snow job* that is tied directly to emotional motivation and it can be used to help you achieve success if you learn
to use it to your advantage. It can win friends and influence people.
It can help you get your Golden Goals by helping others get theirs.

The role of emotional
motivation in success

G. T. Baker, chairman of the board of National Airlines, says:
"The men or women who succeed tomorrow are going to be the ones
who are motivated by a tremendous love of their jobs. . . . Those
who will go far and fast in the space age will owe their success
primarily to their emotional motivation."*

Baker uses the right words and the right music and the simple
fact is that *"love of their work"* (a motivator all its own) is something that today's men and women overlook in their quest for success. They fail to use their hearts as well as their heads in climbing
the pyramids. They fail to use the words that inspire that "love of
their work."

---

* Mel Hickerson, *How to Get What You Want Out of Life* (New York:
Appleton, Century-Crofts, Inc., 1962), p. 19.

The role of emotional motivation in success is sharply plain in the biblical phrase, "As a man thinketh in his heart so is he."

Thinking in your head and believing in your heart are two different things. Yet they are one. For example: It is your conscious mind that does the thinking. It is your conscious mind that listens to words designed to step up your urge for status and the power and glory of success. It's the conscious mind that does the surface thinking. But the watchdog of the soul, the subconscious mind, is the heart of everything. It is the power behind your "hunches" and "instincts." It's an undercover agent working for your welfare on twenty-four hour duty. While the conscious mind sleeps, it works on.

When the subconscious and conscious minds work together, an idea is formed. Desire is created. Determination builds up. Purpose is formulated and everything in and around us begins to build toward success. *The emotionally motivated person works because he HAS to! The motivated person HAS to succeed because words that stimulate him to achievement constantly spur him on.*

If you would succeed YOU have to have this drive, this spur. You have to think with your *heart,* where the word-stimulants find their home. You have to love what you are doing and be packed with enthusiasm to maintain the pace. You have to be wholly committed to the achievement of your dream. When you have this you are on your way!

What is motivation?

Motivation is power. It's the sparkplug that fires you up for the future, the inspirational incentive, the inducement that stimulates emotions, imagination and ability, the incentive which makes you great, the reason for being a human and not a vegetable.

A person seeking success is motivated to success. He is self-propelled by key words that activate him to achievement. These impetus-makers may be triggered by selling-phrases. They may be triggered by praise, flattery, slogans and incentives.

In other words it is key terminology, basic words, that step up someone's desire for success. It's the story of how words become an integral part of the success pattern as told in this chapter. Read this chapter carefully. Study it. Then analyze yourself. Determine what triggers YOU into action. Are you more susceptible to praise than to worldly wealth? Would you rather have a pat on the back than a raise in pay? Is it status quo you want or do you want to move on out and become a dominating power? Do you prefer prestige to security? What motivator stimulates YOU to better performance day after day?

What are motivators?

> *Motivators are emotional hydraulics that lift perform-ance and attitudes above the everyday pattern of per-formance. By themselves they are nothing. As catalysts to human behavior they become powerful propellants in the desire for better performance.*

Motivators are symbolized in key words and phrases such as *"incentive pay," "job advancement," "job security," "retirement."* Other motivator words may be listed as *"challenge," "personal satisfaction," "excellence," "fringe benefits," "bigger take-home pay," "job well done."*

Motivators may also be so basic as the very human need to eat, to drink, to have a home, to seek status, to live in luxury. They may be encapsulated in those three little words "I love you." A *motivator* may be dissatisfaction and discontentment. As you study industry, business and society you will witness motivator words at work. You will see how, as one who learns to use them in executive management or any other phase, you can rise to power, grow in stature, provide others with opportunity for self-growth.

To do this you have to set your words to the music of action. Goals for self-accomplishment, incentives and programs of partici-pation have to be set up and maintained. *The secret to this action is in how you spell out your freedoms from traditional controls, how you soften oppressive rules and regulations, how you help your-self and help others to be accepted, to be eligible for salary raises, to have opportunity for creativity, job safety, love, marriage and thousands of things constantly around you.*

Motivators are ego-influences, personal matters in which the glories of accomplishment are felt, something mastered, some sig-nificant achievement that has been accomplished and the exhilarating thrill which calls for more achievement to replace it. As long as personal satisfaction keeps repeating itself, in the social state of dissatisfied satisfaction, there is no passivity, no boredom. The urge and the surge are forward. The motives that propel this drive are for more achievement, for more security, more prestige, more status, money, and/or affiliation with a group. *You go after these things because you WANT them!* Your ego propels you to get them.

How does motivation work?

No one knows exactly how motivation works. As influences on human behavior, motivators are varied and powerful. They change from time to time. They may change with a person's age. As each motive is satisfied it is replaced with another.

> *A man who has sought security and achieves it seeks status in its place. Another man who has been a success needs repeated successes to be happy. He needs new challenges, something new to master, something to thrill to. He needs to make things happen and this becomes a compulsive and constant action.*

Sometimes motives are hidden. Masks that hide them are often hard to lift. In such people their ability has to be challenged. New stimuli have to be provided and all this may come in the form of words as they reach for success.

Needs may be satisfied with motivating inducements and whether it is a career or a business that is being developed, the incentives and rewards must be plainly marked.

Why does motivation work?

> *Motivation works simply because incentive words propel men to the top of their capacity or the peak of their capability, and as they demonstrate each, to reward them and challenge them further to even better performance than before.*

Motivators are at work when a man becomes excited about his job. They are at work when he finds his job challenging, when he gets satisfaction in working at it, and when detail no longer irks him. When this occurs you have the results of WHY motivation works.

The Five Major Motives
And What They Do

On your flight to success there are particular stimulating words to use on yourself, as well as upon others, and all such motivator words are tied up in the five major motives that impel people to achieve what they want. The five motives are: (1) *Achievement*, (2) *Prestige*, (3) *Security*, (4) *Money*, and, (5) *Affiliation*. These are not only key motivators in executive management but for John Average as well. Let's spend an intimate moment with each in turn.

The achievement motive and
what it does

Key words used in industry to step up the *achievement-motive* are:

Money	Excitement
Power	It's new!
Popularity	Realism
Win	Determination
Goals	Prestige
Achievement	Profit sharing
Forward-motion	Stock in the Company
Challenge	Status
Action	The future
Aggressiveness	Hard work
Be a Boss	Efficiency
Fringe benefits	Recognition
Risk	Overcome obstacles
Effort	Independence
Go-power	Accomplishment etc.

These are samples of motivator words fed from person to person. Such words as these are fed to people who would set the world on fire. Oriented with this type of word men see themselves as winners and they go after the Golden Goals. Such words take them up to king-level in their own eyes.

The achievement motive and where it begins

The *achievement motive* begins in childhood. It is the living result of environmental pressure and the train of events that condition the child for adulthood. It is the desire to reach for something better than the individual already has. To achieve anything better than what he already has he works harder. He fights harder to achieve than do his companions and he puts more effort into it. He demands more of himself. He accepts challenges. Maybe he has a lesser I.Q. but he uses what he has a little harder. He develops his personality and achieves acclaim even while his Phi Beta Kappa friends languish in a lab. He becomes a leader.

The needs of a person who responds to motivation are bigger. Certainly his fight is harder, but his goals to him are more precious. His desire to push himself is strong.

The *achievement motive* makes some people compete harder, but it also gives them a chance to have the fun and excitement of winning. It creates pride in doing something that has not been done before, or doing something better than the next person. It's achievement for achievement's sake rather than for monetary return alone. *Stimulus derived from the competition is more valuable to such a person than any prize he might win.* Money and status thus become secondary assets in his drive for success!

To such a person, rewards, awards and prizes, are of course acceptable. They are acceptable because they are tangible evidence of having won. They are evidence of having "arrived." To such a person profit, as far as money is concerned, is just incidental.

The achievement motive therefore is a force used to guarantee recognition. It is a force used to grease the skids for anything that it is possible to accomplish.

For this reason achievement is a personal matter. It gives a person something he can get in no other way. *He achieves at his own cost despite consequence. He lives to be recognized and applauded.*

Saul W. Gellerman, author of *Motivation and Productivity,* puts it this way — "An achievement-orientated person prefers a moderate degree of risk precisely because his efforts, skills and determination stand a reasonable chance of influencing the outcome. Therefore, the achievement—if there is to be one—will be personal and not just a lucky break or a foregone conclusion. . . . For this reason he prefers activities where feedback is prompt, precise and unmistakable."*

The "feedback" of which Gellerman speaks is what you get in return after having administered praise or compliments, for example. It's the goodwill and rapport which you generate through words. "Feedback" thus becomes something very vital to maintain in stepping up the *achievement motive.* In administering motivator words that generate "feedback" you personally can assure your own success!

Why? Because, through words, you have learned to stimulate people to new highs. You have learned to double your efficiency. By knowing this, says Gellerman, "You can proceed to provide specific task-relevant feedback to the achievement-motivated people and social or 'attitudinal' feedback to the affiliation-motivated people."**

People desire praise

In using words to get achievement-motivated people into motion, remember that the big secret to stimulating them lies in praise whenever possible. PEOPLE NEED PRAISE! Such people who are stimulated by praise are neither aware of hard work nor resentful of it. Such people will work harder and longer than others. They will be more likely to make greater use of their talents. They won't ask you to overcome their personal obstacles. They'll do it themselves!

How do you recognize the achievement oriented person?

1. He is aware of his obstacles but not worried by them.
2. He expects to get recognized for a job well done.

---

* Saul W. Gellerman, *Motivation and Productivity* (American Management Association), p. 126.
** Ibid.

3. He pours his entire resources into gaining success.
4. He accepts challenges no matter what the obstacle.
5. He moves where angels fear to tread.
6. He glories in body and mental contact with odds and expects to come up a winner.
7. He likes to win.
8. His temperament is designed to compete.
9. He likes tasks and getting jobs done where there is a possibility of risk and failure but it isn't too great.

When you excite achievement-orientated people to action through words you are exciting action-minded people. You are setting into motion individuals who are realistic, inventive and demonstrate initiative. When such a person is praised or rewarded, his performance becomes inspirational. He is more aggressive and more determined. He goes for the bigger bonuses and better rewards. To get him to do this you *simply take advantage of his drives and urgencies through words and recognition*. If YOU are the one being motivated you will react the same way.

WORDS TO THE WISE: The people who are most likely to react to persuasive words are the professional people, the salaried people, sales people, executive management and merchants. Take it from there.

The Prestige Motive And How To Take Advantage Of It

In gaining power over people through what you say and do to influence them, remember this one great secret to personal success: *All persons want some form of recognition. They want status! They want prestige! They want personalized attention!*

All of this is a natural want. It's human. It has been a want since time began. It has been a want since words began.

Prestige is an area of respect

Before the desire for prestige is a human want it has to bestowed BY people. If you would manipulate humanity through words, and propagandize them into your way of thinking, you have to manipulate them to higher echelons, to display more approved conduct, to win respect. You have to incite or excite them with what they can expect as they reach higher and higher places on the social, professional, business or industrial pyramid.

Whether you are calling upon one of the church brethren to become a deacon or for a go-go girl to become a mother hen to a nightclub full of chicks the story's the same. Word-power works at all levels. To be looked up to and have prestige is every person's desire.

Prestige motivation is a dominating power, a driving force. It shapes careers. It shapes social and business pyramid climbers and the people who would possess things that the Joneses do not yet have.

What is necessary to stimulate prestige-motivated people?

> *To help people achieve*
> *THEIR WANTS as well as*
> *YOUR GAIN:*
>
> 1. *Work on their pride.*
> 2. *Develop strongly competitive procedures.*
> 3. *Offer rapid advancement.*
> 4. *Offer high-sounding titles.*
> 5. *Add fringe benefits.*
> 6. *Expose such people to future objectives that remain to be accomplished.*

The object, in controlling the prestige-motivated person, is to keep him irresistibly drawn to new goals! Motivate such people to work beneficially for your cause and you simply can't lose! Use the listed six factors to help them achieve their wants. Do this and you also gain.

The Security Motive
And Why It Is Vital To Success

Everyone wants to feel wanted, to be loved. But even more than that they want to feel secure. Security and money are not the same. Yet they are intimately tied. All of us need to feel safe. We need the feeling of protection. To develop this security society creates rules and regulations. From the moment of birth these laws shape us as we adapt to environment.

To get this security the security-motivated person cultivates charm and a *million-dollar personality*. He makes an overt effort to be affable, to be tolerant, so that he can be safe in the future. He wants to build a better and more likable image. He disciplines himself to conform.

As a result of restricting himself the security-motivated person never becomes an entrepreneur, never an innovator, seldom a gambler. Instead he is a "joiner." He finds comfort in being with people and living like the Joneses. As a follower, rather than a leader, he resents change. He resents variation from the rules he learned and although he hides it very well, he does not have a great deal of faith in anything.

The security-motivated person is usually a "nice guy." He is pleasant, non-complaining, patient. Because he doesn't get flustered under pressure he maintains a certain amount of calmness during stress. For him there's pie in the sky mañana and tomorrow will be full of rainbows.

Some break loose from this man-made trap and become leaders. Some become adventurous and start moving outside the walls of safety in a precise effort to reach the Golden Goals. Some refuse to abide by tradition any longer. Some become heroes in time of emergency or war. Some move on out and become winners.

If you have been a security-motivated person all your life, you CAN move on out. If you want more than security, if you want pleasures of not just living securely with people but earning their attention, then you can open the pipeline to their attention through communication.

Turn it on! Communicate! Get through to people! Increase your facility with words and note how you respond to challenge, how you are beginning to enjoy life, how competition is becoming fun, how you're walking the sunny side of the street where the winners walk because they learned to turn it on!

Small Indian can
make heap big talk

Success depends on using the right words in the right place at the right time. Popularity, power, prestige, promotion, status, executive position, command, top dollar, even happiness, depend on getting through to people. Small Indians can learn to make heap big talk and achieve the notice leading to becoming chiefs.

Those who become more engagingly fluent and adept with words are those to whom the Golden Goals go. They are the ones who win and influence people. They find pleasure in self-expression. If you are currently a small Indian you can learn BIG TALK. If you are a chief, your adeptness with words must continue to grow.

The Prestige Motive
And Why It Is Vital To Success

Everyone, at one time or another, has been hungry to be "top dog." Everyone wants a position where he is respected and "looked up to." It's the desire and the expectation of being treated with the best of everything.

Some people want the prestige of being leaders and there are many varieties and levels of leaders. Some are bosses. Some are "straw bosses" and status varies with each. The straw boss wants to become boss, so he works for the new title. He is motivated by the desire for a higher notch, a more prominent position of importance, a wider spread of esteem.

Dissatisfaction underlies the driving necessity to move up in any industry or social environment. Pride is involved and as long as the prestige drive continues the person moves closer and closer to success. Such a person finally levels off at any plateau he desires.

The Money Motive
And Why It Is Vital To Success

Money, with the status symbols it buys, is a strong motivator. To some people money is everything. It is success. To others it is nothing and to them success comes in other ways. To most people the possession of money alleviates the frustrations of being a have-not. It is a stage prop, a monument to be idolized because it represents possession and power and makes men appear to be big in the eyes of their peers.

As the vehicle to bigger and better goals money has become the passport to happiness, a medium of exchange for position, security, and the tangibles of "having arrived."

To acquire this money a person has to keep his services healthy as a marketable commodity if he would continue to raise his standard of living. He has to have an optimistic eye on the future and a desire to improve his station. As his spending power grows, with each new salary increase the want for more money grows. The want for the next higher level of achievement and possession then begins until it is an obsession.

From rowboat pocketbooks one goes to the outboard motor, then the inboard craft and finally the large pleasure craft that sleeps an entire party. The larger possession brings on the "feel of opulence." It gives status. It gives social position as well as a feeling of pride and well-being. This feeling continues until aging, growing cost of operations, and loss of desire set in.

To the "have-nots" money is desirable. To the "haves" it begins to lose its meaning as high tax structures steal it away, leaving nothing but a symbol. As a result, men on the way up shoot for the symbols of leadership and the money is a fringe benefit. They shoot for executive power rather than financial compensation which is taxed away.

There is no uniformity in the money motive but there IS an attitude toward money. This attitude is identified immediately in how a person spends or saves it, how he uses it to become independent of people or to attract their attention.

Money needs are strong. Because money has come to symbolize most tangibles that can be bought, it has become a national hunger. The longing for money, and the security which it is supposed to bring is forever. It is the pad against adversity, the shelter against old age, the medium for buying prestige goods, and as such is much sought and idolized, even though money has no real value of its own.

If you would use words to get at people and that which motivates them you have to play on their motivators. Through words you have to invade their lives. You have to pull on their heart strings, their vanity and their pride. You have to play the game of "They Want" and then help them get it.

I have given you the barest and roughest of evaluations of the chief motivators that run human lives. They are not distinct or clear concepts because there are no distinct or clear concepts, but they *do* give you a handle to hold in your determination to win friends and influence people and talk your way to success. They *do* help you to understand that the emotionally motivated person works because he HAS to. They help you to understand that the motivated person HAS to succeed because it is words that stimulate him to achievement.

Use the encapsulate powers of the great motivators! Use them on yourself as the sparkplugs that fire you up for the future! Become self-propelled as the subconscious message activates you to a course of action. Use the motivators as catalysts to human behavior. Use these powerful propellants to achieve everything you've ever wanted!

10

How To Break The Social Sound Barrier

Day-after-day success depends on breaking the social sound barriers. It depends on using the universal solvent of conversation as you walk the bridge of friendship or business. As a method of self-expression it provides a way to grow, an avenue to rapport, and there's no better approach than words.

E veryone loses when the game of conversation is poorly played. If you break the social sound barriers with ideas and speak up with an interesting well modulated voice that is distinct and clear, if your vocabulary clarifies the idea and puts across the point, then people will find you interesting. If you use words to create a feeling of understanding, of appreciation, of being sympathetic, then you will have created that social bridge called "empathy." You will have developed another aspect of your *Impression Circle.*

The sooner you begin to play the social game of better conversation the sooner you will find yourself drawing closer not only to profit and power but to a *million-dollar personality* as well. How you handle the rules of the game are up to you.

How To Use Conversation
To Its Fullest Advantage

What is conversation?

Conversation, as local color and sentence structure in kodachrome, is a composition of dramatic sounds which distinguish one person from another so that he conveys his personality and his ideas through what he has to say. People like or dislike you in accordance with what they see or hear.

What does conversation do?

In a very specialized manner, conversation is a vehicle to convey understanding, education, and experience. It is a method of creating word pictures with a vocal paintbrush. It is an efficient method of social intercourse in which people get to know you.

With this in mind, it must be noted that unsuccessful people are invariably those who are conversationally inadequate. They are notoriously inarticulate. Their pronunciation, their ill choice of words, their tactlessness in the appropriate use of language, their inability to brighten dark facts with imaginative word pictures, their insecure social ties, make them failures. They predestine social suicide.

Quite often people who want success are stymied by their inability to know what to do with words in carrying on a conversation. Quite often these same people do not realize that conversation makes up a tenth of their personality. As such, conversation plays a decisive role in success and this is notable in men who fail to move up the promotional tree because their talents can't find expressive outlet.

You've seen it over and over: the physician who spends years in college and then hides in a hospital or laboratory because he doesn't know how to get through to people; the handsome dancer who never became a leading man because he "couldn't talk right"; the company man who sits silent at conference tables listening to the stupidity around him, but his own brilliant solutions to their problems die aborning because he hasn't the facility to express them. You've seen it! I've seen it!

Poor conversational ability is not only impractical; it is a handicap. It is a bald admission of social and mental immaturity.

How to develop the art of conversation

There's a time and a place for conversation. There's a time to talk and a time for silence. Many people know how to say nothing, but too few of them know when. Sometimes people misinterpret what they see or hear because it isn't within the scope of their understanding. Perhaps the other person did not "get through." The end result is misunderstanding.

It's a lot like the two Eskimos who were watching construction of a lighthouse on a dangerous Alaskan coast. Construction concluded and a heavy fog rolled in. One Eskimo turned triumphantly to the other and said: "I told you it's no good. The lights shine, the bell dings, the horn blows, but the fog still keeps rolling in!"

Sometimes we build words and conversation into lighthouses and people misinterpret them. Sometimes we talk when silence would be more effective. The thing opened most often by mistake is the human mouth, and this is not the way to break the social sound barrier.

How do you know when
your conversation's right?

Conversation is right when you're not monopolizing it. It's right when you are staying on target and not just chattering. It's right when you can ask yourself the following questions and be positive.

When in doubt about your
conversation ask yourself:
1. Is what I have to say worth listening to?
2. Is this conversation getting anywhere?
3. Is it worthwhile?
4. Is it accomplishing something for somebody?
5. Will it aid my career or achieve an objective?
6. Am I using it as a step up to success?
7. As I using my voice expressively and effectively to create the aura of my *Impression Circle?*
8. Am I developing the showmanship of a *"million-dollar personality"* through the vehicle of my voice?
9. Am I helping someone and hurting no one?
10. Am I getting through to people?

These are simple but very personal questions to the person who is intimately concerned with being a success. They are vital questions to the person interested in using words as the vehicle to his Golden Goals.

Use such questions on yourself! Determine whether your conversation is right. Peek inside your words day after day. Evaluate them. Are they wasting time? Are they accomplishing something? Are they creating a bridge to happier living? Are you using words as an opportunity to find a better life?

How do you handle dull people?

Never stoop down to the level of dullness around you. Remain vivacious despite the Gray People of Obscurity Street around you. Remember, too, that people who appear dull are not always from Dullsville. It could very readily be that the fault is yours. You simply haven't expressed yourself understandably. You haven't gotten through. To get through faster, always touch people where they are socially sensitive. Determine their likes, their wants. Probe not just their interests but their pride. Move in gracefully by using conversational openers such as the following.

*Suggestions for getting
the other person to
"open up":*

1. "I'd like your opinion on. . . ."
2. "What is your advice about . . ."
3. "I understand that . . ."
4. "That reminds me about the time that . . ."
5. "Would you take a look at that!"

Purposefully, tactfully, you open the door. If you are not adept in the art of conversation, keep working at it. Develop the art of word-sculpturing, because you may have been living in Dullsville. You, too, may have a need to come conversationally awake.

To be a better conversationalist you need something to talk about. You can supply this need by reading, by research, travel and experience. You can develop a scrapbook of clippings and keep up on that which is current. You can develop a conversational file as do I. This is my "inside information" that keeps me aware of the characteristics and habits of people, as well as what they are doing. Such information is of interest. More than this, it is a better way to understand them. Such a scrapbook keeps you mentally alert to that which is around you. The "inside information" gives you informed advantage.

When in Rome do as . . .

Always talk at the level your listener understands. When you're with extraordinary people don't use ordinary words. Use sculptured, colorful words that tell a story, descriptive words that sparkle and gleam. Create living portraits with words that have the sight and sound of intellect. When you are with people of lesser mental stature, diplomatically, unobtrusively, and gently seek out their areas of interest. Converse about the things which they know best.

Give them the chance to tell THEIR story, because it's the most beautiful story ever told . . . by them!

Vocal Dynamics:
Your Pathway to Power

One of the first steps in making vocal contact is to have something interesting about which to talk. So encourage people to talk. Determine their interests. Let them express their ideas and opinions. Please them by asking their advice. Be enthusiastic as you talk about that which is of most interest to them. THEN, get your message across, and be enthusiastic about it!

HOW TO RECOGNIZE
AN ENTHUSIASTIC PERSON

1. *An enthusiastic person* has tomorrow in view because he has completely forgotten yesterday.

2. *An enthusiastic person* is exuberant and vivacious. He sees no clouds on the dullest days.

3. *An enthusiastic person* makes people happy. As a result he draws them into his aura of personal magic.

4. *An enthusiastic person* is never personal.

5. *An enthusiastic person* looks you in the eye and simply expresses himself.

6. *An enthusiastic person* is stimulating and infectious and if you remain in his presence it isn't long before you are acting the same way.

7. *An enthusiastic person* shares and compares his experiences with people.

8. *An enthusiastic person* talks *briefly* about his hobbies.

9. *An enthusiastic person* says just enough to "draw out" the other person. He determines their interests, which may be one and the same with his. If he is a theatre buff he swings conversation in this direction. If this

try doesn't touch first base, he veers to art, books, television, sports, current events, outstanding places, etc.

10. *An enthusiastic person* at no time ever speaks negatively of anyone.

YOU can be an extraordinary person by being an enthusiastic person in conversation. YOU too can be vivacious and expressive. YOU can be stimulating to others and have an infectious personality. YOU too can wrap people up in the bright music of words and assure your own success. YOU can create tomorrow through enthusiastic conversation today. You can use enthusiasm as a method of adapting to people . . . and make it pay.

Develop the social cohesion of "adaptation" through conversation

Adaptation is a conscious modification of your adjustment to the social environment around you. It is constantly necessary to adapt to every person you meet. Each person demands a different approach, a change of pace. Each person demands conversation pointed strictly at HIM.

Adaptation, therefore, demands complete flexibility on your part if you would develop social cohesion in this effort to make people like you, in this effort to talk your way to success.

With this in mind, consciously go about adapting a friendly attitude even toward those who repel you. Simply refuse to be repelled. Find something, no matter what, about that person that can be admired.

Dig for it through conversation with him. Find it. Praise him for it and watch a phenomenon take place. You will have opened up a glorious new page in friendship because you took the time to adapt. You took another step closer to success as the result of words.

Each time you adapt to a new person, a new character, a new personality, you will find yourself growing more self-reliant, more proficient, more capable. You will no longer be short-circuited by your inability to get through to where people live intimately within themselves.

What do you eliminate
to be socially acceptable?

To assure the process of adaptation, you have to eliminate your hates, your dislikes, prejudices and irritations. These are the tension-makers. They are the social sound barriers between people when there is no need for them to exist. There is no need to be critical, but there IS a need to be understanding and friendly. See a friend in every stranger and in every race and creed, and barriers will never exist!

Recognize your sound barriers

There are many kinds of social sound barriers. One of them is silence. One of them is the act of talking too much. One may be gossiping or being the possessor of odd vocal or physical mannerisms that make conversation difficult to maintain. Such mannerisms may be repellent.

Despite these mannerisms in others, refuse to be repelled. Never be repelled by vulgarity or tactlessness. Instead be temporarily attracted to people whose ideas and way of life are alien to yours. Before you depart from their presence you will have learned something other then vulgarity. Know them! Understand them!

I recall a magazine writing assignment where I had to investigate that social phenomenon, that rebellion of youth, called the "hippies." I lived with them. I lived in squalor and came away with a new understanding. I came away with something I would not have had without first-hand experience.

On another assignment I joined a factory working crew. They went out on strike. I had been instructed not to go out. As a result they beat the hell out of me. I found out why the hard way.

Adapt! Bargain! Don't shut other people out of your life. As you do this you will begin to find that your tolerance is growing, that you are growing socially, that you are becoming more proficient and capable in handling people through words, that you are becoming more impersonal in your judgments and less bound by tradition, that as a result of all this you are more and more able to talk your way to success.

Too often we reject people because we see them in moments of stress and embarrassment, and if you would see yourself in the same light, look into a mirror during an angry moment. See the savage that's there. See something that is not socially adaptable and is not desirable. So instead of rejecting people and passing false judgments, welcome them into your life! You don't have to live with them. But you do need understanding of that which makes them click.

Once you adjust your attitude, your thinking and your conversation you will be more compatible with all kinds of people. In your effort to control a career, or control people through the power and persuasion of words, you must first control yourself. Remember that *that which you resent in others may be the same trait that you resent in yourself.*

Beware of the subtle traps

Be warned in advance that there are traps into which word-users fall. They're subtle traps. Such traps are everywhere. The signposts on them say: "Button your lip!" These are the traps into which you fall when you inadvisably use words that violate someone's preconceived ideas or jar their fears awake. These are the traps where you hurt someone's feelings or pride, traps where you unwittingly dent someone's attitudes or opinions.

> *In using words to achieve success, become more and more aware of the attitudes in other people. Become conscious of opinion and emotion, of wants and urges. All such factors shape the lives of people and their desires. They shape their occupations, their religions, their illnesses and their health. They shape the minds of executive management as well as the minds of those who labor in the plant. In one way or another everyone is intolerant, everyone is prejudiced or shows bias. If you would be a success through the diplomatic use of words, beware of the booby-traps in conversation that can explode with vicious repercussion.*

The majority of people become unreasoning under stress. Too few have vision or imagination that they can productively use. Too few have solid interests or belief. For this reason YOU HAVE TO SUPPLY A NEED! In supplying this need you also have to avoid the subtle traps and package yourself as a well designed product to fill their want.

On February 22, 1967, the late Senator Robert Kennedy said: "As our population increases, as the problems of our society become more complex and as the cost of political campaigns continues to mount, it becomes more and more clear that the package is often more important than the product, that the perceived image of a candidate is more important than what he says."

How To Avoid
The Word Traps

At no time permit yourself to argue, dispute, contradict, or enter any human zone of emotional privacy.

Why fight ideas that are preconceived? Why argue with status quo when there are other dynamic ways to handle them? Why entangle yourself in webs of intolerance and hate? Why rob yourself of prestige? Why let the lifeblood of success go down the drain because you flushed yourself out of the sight and sound of people by losing their faith in you, their confidence and their respect?

How, then, do you handle the word traps? Simply recognize them for what they are. Then let them slide past unchallenged even as you acknowledge them to yourself. For specific examples of how to avoid the word traps from A to Z, here are twenty-six ways to do it:

**Straight tips on coping
with word traps**

   a. *Don't gossip. Smile gently. Shrug. Walk away.*
   b. *Don't admit you know nothing about controversial situations.*
      When you are hit with a point-blank question on a delicate matter, just hide behind another question: "How do YOU feel about the matter, Mrs. Jones?" All right, so you've sidestepped. You've remained unin-

volved. So what have you accomplished? *You have given the other person opportunity to say what he has been bursting to say in the first place.* This is diplomacy in words. It is economy of effort. It is mastery of a situation and if you would be master of every situation, take advantage of the opportunity that each presents. Do it by *buttoning your lip* at the right time!

c. *Recognize that the other person has feelings.*

d. *Recognize that he has an opinion.*

e. *Give him a chance to voice his opinion.*

f. *Help him believe he is more than just a no-talent person.*

g. *Take him off guard by saying the unexpected.*

h. *Agree with him.* That, too, he doesn't expect.

i. *Never challenge his self-repect.*

j. *At no time permit bias or prejudice to enter the picture.*

k. *Never attempt to "get even."*

l. *Walk away from all high-tension problems.* Collect yourself. Come back later when you're calm.

m. *Make deliberate effort to be more than fair.*

n. *Be generous. Be charitable.*

o. *Be courteous.*

p. *Insulate yourself against social nastiness of others.*

q. *Talk only of good things.* Avoid the bad and unfavorable.

r. *Never be the one who carries bad news.* Let John do it.

s. *Retain high-level honesty.*

t. *Praise people lavishly.*

u. *Be sincere.*

v. *Give freely to those who need your help.*

w. *Never discredit anyone* or speak disparagingly.

x. *Say you are happy to see and meet people.*

y. *Say nothing detrimental about anyone who is absent.*

z. *Make your voice portray and dramatize your pleasure.*

What are the major traps to avoid?

The twenty-six factors listed above indicate an *approach* to the word traps. Now we have to put our finger on specifics and avoid them. Remember that all word traps are social traps. They happen at the point of contact despite the fact that they come prefabricated out of the past. Such traps are defined. Recognize them. Know them for what they are. Label them with the message—"NO TRESPASSING." In chart form here are the specific danger areas to delete from your conversation:

Specific Word Traps in Conversation		
Number One Trouble Spots	**Number Two Trouble Spots**	**Number Three Trouble Spots**
Don't discuss:	*Beware discussing:*	*Avoid discussing:*
Divorce	Relatives	Details on anything
Separation	Appearance of	Taste in clothing
Sex (vulgarities)	others	Vices or bad social
Non-achievement	Personal likes or	habits of others
Choice of friends	dislikes	Someone's play for
Religion	Personal superiority	sympathy or pity
Politics	Mental handicaps	What you have
Someone's "affairs"	of others	done for some-
Business during	Illness or operations	one
meals		Cost of clothing,
Gossip		home, etc.

There are many other word traps of which you will become aware if you are truly interested in using words as a method to achieve success. You will learn to exclude, for example, conversation that excludes someone in the immediate group. You will avoid such personalized remarks as, "Why she's so skinny that every time she drinks coffee she looks like a thermometer," or "Why doesn't she wear falsies? Every time she wears black her chest looks like two pimples on a blackboard."

Disparagement like this is a sadistic and cruel form of humor. It serves only to alienate the listener. It also reminds him that the same vitriolic tongue may be turned on him. The point is, in influencing people through conversation, don't put them on defense. *Never make them ill at ease or embarrassed in your presence.* Be agreeable instead. *Refuse to be emotionally, argumentatively, or critically involved.* Simply refuse to be a vindictive gossip or shrew.

If you are saying "Well, what does that leave me to talk about?" then you need to re-examine yourself in your relationship with humanity. You have failed to read the "no trespassing" signs. You have fallen into the word traps and this is always at the cost of your personal relationship with people. It is at the cost of personality and at the cost of personal achievement. You simply haven't used the opportunity that conversation gives you in talking yourself *up* to success.

Restyling designs for breaking the sound barrier

Because of social, professional and business pressures your thinking may be distorted by emotions at times. To all such emotional upheavals brakes have to be applied. Sometimes we are unaware of our emotional trigger areas that make us conversationally undesirable. To help you put your finger on *your* possible trigger zones, the list on page 132 is a depth probe to sound them out.

To prevent the immature reactions listed here, learn to accept stress. Develop healthy attitudes. In the face of healthy attitudes unhealthy attitudes retreat. In the face of strength of purpose, emotional sabotage can be neutralized. Your thinking becomes less hampered, less obstructed. To bring about this change *it is necessary to retrain your mental attitudes.* It is necessary to develop inhibiting controls and healthy reactions.

EMOTIONAL AREAS
TO AVOID IF YOU WOULD
BREAK THE SOUND BARRIER

*Check in factors
of which YOU
are guilty:*

	Yes No		Yes No
1. Alibis	.. ..	35. Misconceptions	.. ..
2. Anxiety	.. ..	36. Uncompromising	.. ..
3. Apathy	.. ..	37. Poor loser	.. ..
4. Avoiding duties	.. ..	38. Prejudice	.. ..
5. Anger	.. ..	39. Packed with envy	.. ..
6. Being without faith	.. ..	40. Posing	.. ..
7. Being highly biased	.. ..	41. Ridicule	.. ..
8. Boasting	.. ..	42. Revenge	.. ..
9. Bullying	.. ..	43. Sarcasm	.. ..
10. Cheating	.. ..	44. Saving face	.. ..
11. Constant fatigue	.. ..	45. Selfishness	.. ..
12. Cowardice	.. ..	46. Self-centeredness	.. ..
13. Defeatist attitude	.. ..	47. Self-pity	.. ..
14. Discontentment	.. ..	48. Succumbing to	
15. Dishonesty	.. ..	temptation	.. ..
16. Fear	.. ..	49. Seeking sympathy	.. ..
17. Feeling inferior	.. ..	50. Stalling	.. ..
18. "Getting even"	.. ..	51. Speaking disparag-	
19. Gloating	.. ..	ingly of others	.. ..
20. Hatred	.. ..	52. Temper tantrums	.. ..
21. Insecurity	.. ..	53. Uncontrolled	
22. Intolerance	.. ..	ambition	.. ..
23. Indecision	.. ..	54. Untruth	.. ..
24. Irresponsiblity	.. ..	55. Wild cursing	.. ..
25. Insincerity	.. ..	56. Without hope	.. ..
26. Lack of ambition	.. ..	57. Without confidence	.. ..
27. Lack of dignity	.. ..	58. Without	
28. Lack of courtesy	.. ..	understanding	.. ..
29. Lack of conscience	.. ..	59. Worry	.. ..
30. Lack of goals	.. ..	NOTE:	
31. Lack of respect	.. ..	Deliberately go about de-	
32. Lack of sympathy	.. ..	leting these trigger zones day	
33. Lack of patience	.. ..	after day!	
34. Lying	.. ..		

Attitudes Can Be Changed!

Attitudes are not changed by KNOWING what to do about them. They are changed by thinking and DOING what is necessary to bring about change!

Attitudes Are Changed by:

1. Retraining an idea or attitude
2. Removing offensive memories
3. Recognizing personal trigger zones
4. Knowing your susceptibility to stress
5. Being conscious of your emotional threshold
6. Controlling your tensions
7. Giving good attitudes daily outlet

Meet negative attitudes head-on! Meet and recognize them for what they are! Accept their challenge. Understand them. Then work them over to suit your purpose. Change your attitudes, where necessary, to meet circumstance. Keep constantly adaptable as you talk your way to success. Just don't argue!

How To Handle Arguments

Thirty-one sure ways to handle irate people

What's the technique for handling an angry person with words? There's not just one way to do it. There are many. Learn them. Fit them to the situation. Here are thirty-one ways now to make yourself look ten feet tall to the other person after he has cooled off.

Techniques:

1. *Tell him he's entirely right!*

   Agree. This will stop him cold. Agree with him and there's no place else for him to go. So give him attention and not an argument. Listen intently to what he has to say because his biggest problem is the need for sympathy and understanding.

2. *Permit him to deliver his tirade unopposed.*

   When he's shot his wad, tell him you believe you understand his problem but, "Would you please repeat it so that I can understand just a little bit better." The moment he begins to repeat his argument it will dwindle away. Anger will be spent because, in his growing awkwardness, he is now realizing that his argument is mostly anger and noise. So be diplomatic. Let him tell his story. *Use listening as a strategic move to establish control.*

3. *Walk away from arguments*

   Why squander the possibility of success by becoming involved in that which is inconsequential and destructive? Walk away!

4. *Never argue!*

   No argument is ever logical. You lose even with winning. In its place, what social facility do you use? Use words that appeal to the other person's vanity and pride. Be lavish with praise. Say to that person: "Kingston, that's a great idea! I would never have thought of it. You're a credit to the company!"

5. *Never permit emotions to influence you*

   By remaining emotionally removed from emotional stress areas you never get involved in fruitless arguments. Simply provide no fuel for the other person to burn.

6. *Don't permit argumentative situations to rise in the first place*

   Keep others from getting dismayed, confused, hurt or belligerent. Keep them happy and arguments won't happen.

7. *Forget remarks designed to "cut somebody down."*

   Delete all words of sarcasm, disparagement and discouragement out of your vocabulary. Be kind. Be sympathetic. Be understanding. Permit the other person to think that he is right . . . that he has won. Later you can get the social problem under control through diplomacy.

8. *If you have been insulted, forget it!*

   Flatten the other person's offense with a smile. He's got no place to go when you don't argue.

9. *Accept criticism easily.*

   Compliment the other person on his astute observation. Tell him he's entirely right. With the wind gone from his sails, he's standing still with no place to go.

10. *Surprise the person with praise instead of a retaliatory wisecrack.*

11. *Be willing to spend a little time in explanation.*

    Nothing causes people to become irate faster then being deprived or being left outside of something they feel is important or vital to them. Knowledge and understanding is one of these factors. Give them understanding through words.

12. *Let him think his argument is original*

    Permit the other person to think his idea is a "first." Later you can check out the real cause for his problem and his reaction.

13. *Never criticize*

14. *Walk and talk softly in the presence of anger*

    You can stop the other person fast by speaking softer and softer until he can hardly hear you. Of necessity he will have to tone himself down just to hear whether you are participating in the argument. Keep in mind at all times that *your point of view is of no interest to him.*

15. *Answer all questions with more questions*
    Don't get yourself trapped or committed to a position.

There's a time and a place to declare where you stand, but it is NEVER during a time of anger.

16. *Give him something to take away.*

    Say: "Of course, Mr. Jones, we'll be glad to replace the merchandise. We're sorry the machine was defective. To show you our appreciation for being so nice, here's a set of steak knives for your wife."

17. *Let him know you understand*

18. *Give him your fullest wide-eyed attention*

19. *Get close to him. Look him in the eye*

    Light your face with understanding and let him think he's the greatest.

20. *Put a smile on your face and a firm grip in your handshake*

    It takes only twelve muscles to smile, forty-six to frown, so turn the frown upside down and burn less energy.

21. *Talk his language*

    He understands only what he knows. He comprehends only what he understands, so speak in the language he knows.

22. *Keep self-interest out—refuse to be selfish!*

    See the entire picture. Act for the benefit of the majority.

23. *Let the other person voice his contention first!*

24. *Listen! Adapt the other person's idea*

    After you have once sounded him out, you can use his own argument as a lever. Wrap your own theme around it to make it acceptable. This technique can be used over and over to win others to you. *It's a method of apparent capitulation, with yourself unobtrusively in control!* It's diplomacy in words.

25. *Cooperate*

26. *Look at "arguments" as a time loss on your schedule.*
Refuse to devote any time to this type of loss.

27. *Appear forever calm*
Never elevate your voice. No matter whether your blood pressure is up or not refuse to show it. In the face of your calmness others fall into the same condition. Anger is resolved.

28. *Stay in tune with optimism, happiness and forward motion*

29. *Keep positive at all times*
Simply refuse to be depressed, oppressed, discouraged or feel low. Express nothing negative at any time.

30. *NEVER ask people to DO something—don't demand!*
To prevent an argument before it starts always make your requests diplomatically. To get things done without conflict, create questions that provide two choices.

Example:

(a) "Which would you like to do, dear? Take the garbage out or put the baby's diapers in the washing machine?"

(b) "Johnny, do you prefer knocking out the radio spot announcements on the Fraser account or that mailing piece for Kennicutt?"

31. *Never direct your cross fire at the firebrands*
In a conference or crowd, never direct your "arguments" at the shouters and noisier ones. Get the support of the calm and open minds by addressing them. Once you have their support, you can then twist noisy ones' ideas to suit the will of the group. It's social manipulation, but it's a way to talk yourself to success.

How to identify the gossip
whom you must avoid

Earmarks of the gossip:

1. *The gossip* talks about people, not about ideas or things.
2. *The gossip* maintains a constant flow of unending trivia.
3. *The gossip* overuses "He said" and "She said."
4. *The gossip* uses significant silences or mannerisms after raising matters of privacy.
5. *The gossip* delights in making cutting, sarcastic, derisive, abrasive, embarrassing remarks.
6. *The gossip* is quickly bored with conversations that are on subjects other than people.

How do you handle the gossip with words? You don't! You just walk away. Waste neither time nor conversation with anything or anyone malicious. Start being more alert.

How To Develop
The Alert Manner

No one cares to converse with a person who is listless, indifferent, moody, or shows battle fatigue. To prevent becoming equally dull, avoid all people who are not animated by something within them that makes them appear, and act, alert.

Develop the alert manner! Be enthusiastic about everything and let it show. Refuse to be associated with anything, or anyone, who is listless and dull. Remove yourself from the presence of people or environments that are exhausting and repellent. Live and act with lively and active people! Be stimulating to be around! Be enthusiastic. Have a sense of humor and note how magnetic this appeal can be, how your personality comes alive, how you achieve that external glow, that *impression circle!* Note the magic wand it waves and how this magic wand can be dubbed the *million dollar personality**

---

* J. V. Cerney, *How to Develop a Million Dollar Personality* (West Nyack, N.Y.: Parker Publishing Co., 1964).

The moment you adopt the alert manner, and a more vivacious outgoing style of personality, you will find that tiredness drops away. As you convert somber words to words of exuberance and good living you will find yourself brimming with vitality!

Mental attitudes change the endocrine attitude of the body and with hormones in your system you actually zip up your congeniality and better health. You become more interested in people, more understanding of them, as well as more alert.

In becoming more conversationally adept in influencing people, light up *their* enthusiasm as well as your own. To accomplish this speed up your conversational delivery. Show spirit. Arouse interest. Apply the spark that fires them up. Be stimulating. Be colorful without being obnoxious. Talk about matters that are happy and attractive. Avoid mentioning your troubles. Avoid anything and everything you disapprove. Avoid complaints. Simply refuse to be negative about anything!

There is no better way to break through the sound barriers and tie people to you than by using words and attitudes of cheer. Enthusiasm is the Number One asset that endears and attracts and it can be enhanced in all its human forms. Humor may be one such form.

Humor, And The Role
It Plays In Your Life

Direct exposure to people makes them quickly conscious of what you are. Conversation furnishes the link to this discovery.

In today's industrial and business world "bad exposures" means a "poor human relations program." Or it may be interpreted as "bad publicity" or as "inadequate public relations." It may simply mean you are conversationally not up to par. It may mean that you just have no sense of humor.

Words are not only inspirational to others. They are inspirational and health-giving to YOU. Words can get you into trouble or save you from awkward and embarrassing situations. They can deliver you from shyness or shift the balance of feeling superior or inferior. They can create an aura of happiness or social acceptance around you if you desire. They can help you appreciate others and be appreciated by them as you develop social outlet through words.

Words are indeed a powerful outlet. They are powerful motivators as well and it's up to you to use them. It's up to you to use humor as a means to make people laugh.

Humor is a situation that arises naturally out of an incongruity where some absurdity develops in human behavior or character. It's the quality of being funny.

Humor is a strong social control. It often saves a situation when nothing else will. By using the saving grace of humor you not only relieve the stress of emotions but you release self-induced tensions as well.

A dentist friend of mine had a neat way of releasing tension through humor. He did it like this: One day he had a patient in the chair who was very apprehensive. She became more and more tense, despite his assurance that it was a small cavity. Her knuckles were white as her hands gripped the chair arm. Her eyes were screwed shut. Her body was stiff.

"How come, Doctor," she managed to gasp, "that a small cavity feels so large to the tongue?"

"Perhaps," he said quietly, "this is due to the tendency of the tongue to exaggerate."

His humor registered. She started to giggle and then relaxed. He filled the tooth quickly and it was over. "Oh doctor," she said, "you're such a card."

Humor is a business investment

In business it is interesting to note that no man becomes a failure without his own consent. No one becomes a success without developing the saving grace of humor. Humor, cultivated or uncultivated, is a business investment and there's a place for it everywhere.

Pat Lambert of Roesch Motors, always said, "The test of success is showing respect for those who can be of little benefit to you." I believe this, but every time I hear him say it I always think of the forward young man who went to his boss and said, "Sir, since one of the vice presidents of our company has died, why can't I take his place?"

The boss looked the lad over quietly and said, "It's all right with me, Johnny. But I'll have to check with the undertaker first."

The boss could have exploded. He didn't. He simply forgot the seriousness of the situation and the social ineptitude of the boy, and permitted his sense of humor to release the tension. Through words he maintained self-control.

Spontaneous good humor takes fast thinking. It takes adeptness and practice. It takes advantage of humorous situations as they develop. It takes a playful spirit and a nice smile. It takes learning to laugh at one's self as well as seeing the ridiculous in something or in someone else.

Laugh at yourself, but never at your own jokes

As your first business investment in shooting for success, learn to laugh at yourself. Never be so serious about yourself that you become overburdened with it. The moment you start seeing the funny side of anything you are taking a strategic step in the success pattern. So look for things about which to be humorous. Look for surprises and that which is incongruous. Look for that which can be exaggerated with a little twist. It may be a pun, it may be a comparison, but couch the situation in a setting that makes someone laugh.

Let the humor be at your expense. When you use humor, make sure that it fits the occasion. Make sure stories brief and to the point and don't kill the gag by laughing at it yourself. You will only distract your audience's attention from the punch line.

Use humor effectively and you will find yourself establishing a kind of rapport with people that is wholesome and good. You will have indicated, through humor, that you are a down-to-earth, human, and approachable person. Through humor you will have gotten through to people and this is what counts in using words to talk your way to success.

Put people at ease! Relieve their tensions! Never hurt or humiliate! Use humor as the social cohesive that cements the elements of friendship. It's never a mistake to use humor and *success comes to those who profit from the fewest mistakes.*

Success usually comes to those who are too busy to look for it, so they get some laughs along the way. In your particular reach for success, stop being the quiet one. Have fun! Remember that quiet ones aren't the only ones who don't have much to say. Use humor like a challenge. Using humor like a challenge reminds me of the circus strong man who came to our town looking for my Uncle Bill. Uncle Bill was known throughout the state for his prodigious strength.

The circus man came to challenge him. I watched the man ride his horse up inside Uncle Bill's gate. He closed the gate and said: "I heard about you back in town. Now I want to see who's the better man."

Uncle Bill didn't say a word. His big hands whipped out, grabbed the strong man, and hurled him over the gate. He brushed himself off and in his gentle way said, "Anything else you want?"

"Yes," said the stunned circus performer as he broke the sound barrier, "Would you please throw me my horse?"

Developing
The Power-Thrust
To Recognition

In the reach for recognition, as well as for pep, popularity and power, the words you use are subject to misunderstanding and misinterpretation as well. They are subject to innuendo, nuance, changing expression and mood. Words are subject to variations in using them. Because of this it is necessary to discipline and control the words you use. In developing the power-thrust to recognition you have to engineer the command performance of speech.

143

S ome vocal expressions come out of the human mouth flat, dead, without color. Others are resonant, bright, vivacious. They have change of pace, timing, exaltation, excitation and punctuation. The bright, vivacious speaking voice marks the alert person. It marks the person who has *directional control* in his flow to success.

Because there is feeling and meaning in every verbal package of conversation, it has to come on strong to those who are listening. Conversation has to be a positive agent with oral regulation.

To control the direction and meaning of words you have to make them colorfully expressive to command the attention you desire.

In using words to shoot for success permit your body and hands to also become articulate. Let feeling and emotions play a controlled role in directing your gestures. In turn, use words to manipulate the emotions of others.

Like a television transmitter, radiate your emotions, your thoughts and feelings, with full intent to stimulate somebody's thinking, someone's emotions and feelings. Design words to fire up ideas in people as you go.

Johnny Dawson, personnel director of Challenge Industries, has this to say: "In developing the power-thrust to recognition make people glad you're with them. Fill a need in their lives! Find something nice to say about everything and everyone. Be positive at all times. If the salad has garlic in it which you despise, don't mention it to your hostess. Praise the meat instead. Commend people. Show enthusiasm. Bubble with fellowship. Flood people with the fluency of your goodwill toward men. Be attractive. Stimulate them with ideas and word-imagery. Give them happiness and as a fringe benefit you will find your own tensions and pressures easing away. You will find that you have a growing *directional control* of your life."

To direct the behavior of people, animate them with the intensity of your personal drive. Move them to action. Be entertaining if necessary, but be persuasive. Get your message across!

Are you getting
YOUR message across?

The fact that you have a good vocabulary means nothing until you give it persuasive direction. It is valueless until it describes what is in your mind. It is no good until others understand what you have to say and what you say inspires them to act.

Words are fed out in waves or sentences. These waves, on impact with the human ear, become more than information. They become incentives. They become influences on human behavior. When this happens words stimulate action and the accent is on *Personality Appeal*. When this happens the living brain transmits a strong *directional control*. The direction is in your favor.

In feeding words through the pattern of conversation, through song, a public speech or words in a book, it's not always WHAT you say but HOW you say it. Hollywood song teacher Charles Henderson puts it this way, "The accent today is on intimacy."*

It's not always what the message is. It's how you create emotional awareness that makes a bridge of intimacy between yourself and others. When you stop to think about it ARE YOU GETTING YOUR SONG ACROSS?

Some years ago we had an old Indian in our small town who insisted on making moonshine. Twice his still blew up, and the noise, more than the booze, caused the sheriff to tell Joe he had to get out of town. Since there was no place for Joe to go, the citizens bought some wasteland in the county and donated the sand and brush to Joe.

Contentedly he built himself a shanty and went back to running his still again. Two years later a Texas oil company was scouting Michigan. It checked Joe's sand pit and set up a drilling rig. A gusher was hit. Joe grew rich. He continued to live in the same shack and continued to make moonshine, but now he had a Cadillac. On the Cadillac he rigged four horns of different sounds and volume which he blared wildly as he rode up and down the county roads at four o'clock in the morning. To show his utter contempt for the local citizens he not only tormented them with noise but he deliberately ran his Cadillacs off the bridge and into the river. Then he'd go buy a new one.

---

* Charles Henderson and Charles Palmer, *How to Sing for Money* (Chicago: Nelson-Hall Co., 1945), p. 4.

No one could get through to Joe that this was not the thing to do. No one got the song across until a little old lady by the name of Molly Durrell went out to his house with fresh soup and bread when she heard he was sick.

Joe was taciturn and suspicious until she said, "Joe, give people the chance to like you."

It was what she said and how she put it across that made Joe become a solid citizen. He began buying his booze instead of making it. His Cadillac became a van for carting Boy Scouts to summer camp. Molly Durrell got HER song across when everyone else failed.

Where are you putting YOUR accent?

Have you ever stopped to think that *it isn't WHAT you say but HOW you say it?* That the accent on intimacy is strong?

How is this ability developed? How do you learn to get through to people on a more intimate basis so that your words are giving them *directional control?*

First you have to take the idea that this is possible and you begin to work at it. You use the magic power of words. You talk "naturally." You talk of things that penetrate their tender zones. You talk "sense." You talk colorfully and vivaciously. You put your accent on *Personality Appeal* and become fluent with it as you sway people through words.

To become a modern Sophocles or Demosthenes you have to set up a rehearsal time each day. You have to lose self-consciousness through practice. Be completely conscious of words as you learn to manipulate people and events to your purpose. You develop quality control and technique of usage. You develop flair with words and create quality instead of quantity. If you are an author you learn to do this on a typewriter. If you are a thespian you do it on the stage. In everyday life the world is your stage on which you play to a full time audience. It is our laboratory to try the many procedures in this book.

With this fluency comes something new. With it comes the HOW, the rendition, the tone and technique of delivery. When this happens you are on your way to getting across your "hard or soft sell." The accent is on intimacy.

When you put words together logically and express them logically you create a message. People recognize messages in accordance with their ability to understand them. Whether you speak jargon or a common language you have to be understood. You have to invite interest in what you have to say. You have to gain attention and this comes only in the HOW of conversational release. It comes only with getting your song across. When you start "getting through" to people you are developing your power-thrust to recognition.

To gain recognition what you have to say has to be exciting. It has to be packed with incentive. It must probe consciences or irritate. It must proclaim you to the world.

In all cases, words, as directives, must be said with intent to get something, to do something, and to bring about action! They must be channeled and controlled to gain the maximum benefit from their power-thrust!

Simple and strong words can do a selling job for you

England's Prime Minister Winston Churchill said in a time of war, "I have nothing to offer but blood, toil, tears and sweat."

Twenty years later, during his presidential inaugural address on January 20, 1961, John F. Kennedy said, ". . . *my fellow Americans, ask not what your country can do for you; ask what you can do for your country.*"

These are simple words, strong words, words that stimulate compelling pictures and even more compelling action. These men created words that will never die. They created living messages, messages that spoke out to people with something more than words. This was the HOW of words when there was a necessity for common response. The need in war was for action. The need in peacetime was for action of another kind. Words were used to speak out with intent to unify conflicting impulses and interests of others. According to Karl Deutsch, "Communication is the cement that makes organizations."* Communication is the cement that holds families as well as nations or business places together. Words are a powerful cohesive indeed.

The appeal of President Kennedy and Prime Minister Churchill is no different than the "how" used by executive management in industry. They appealed to people. They used the strategy of words to create results.

If you would develop the strategy of gaining recognition throguh the power-thrust of words you have to use the words that ring bells and open doors. The words have to be designed to achieve a goal.

I call this the *forward-thrust* of words. It's a *forward-thrust* channeled to contain the listener in the environment of an idea. In this *forward-thrust*, this power-thrust, you utilize words that are attention-getters. You stimulate desire to cooperate. You cut down opponents by stimulating their wants. You stimulate their pride. You mold opinion and purposefully channel people into areas where they are responsive. When this happens you are in the driver's seat. You have *directional control*. Keep cognizant of the two big actions: *forward-thrust* and *directional control*. They are your answer to success tomorrow.

Through words man becomes a force. He uses words in planning. He uses words in programming the future for himself and for others. He finds that his facility for influencing people grows. So does his capability for becoming successful. The moment he is conscious of this phenomenon he becomes more able to compute his probability for success.

> *By effectively controlling words you can control your power as a person, your strategy as a person wanting recognition, your future if you would be a success. In direct proportion to the dynamics of your power-thrust develops your capability for effecting recognition.*

Tomorrow is controlled
by the song you sing today

How well you learn to direct the *forward-thrust* of words and their *directional control* determines all fringe benefits as well as

---

* Karl Deutsch, "Communication Theory and Social Science," *Selected Papers on Psychotherapy, Purpose and Communication* (New York: American Orthopsychiatric Association, 1952), p. 470.

success in the future. Words are the magic thread in your life, your roadway to tomorrow, so the words you use and the song you sing must be sung with success in view.

How well you control the volatile dynamic power of words predetermines success and this cannot be repeated often enough. How well you utilize the encapsulated power of words and their limitless energy determines your future. Communication, as the lifeblood of progress, determines your success.

How To Develop A Blueprint For Action

Words, as indicated over and over, generate power. They are verbal energy formulated to twist circumstance to advantage and through planned strategy you manipulate *forward-thrust + directional control* so that it comes out in the pattern you desire. To develop your pattern you have to set up an original guideline. This pattern, formula, or guideline, is then applied to the industry, occupation or kind of life in which you are seeking success.

> *A minister's pattern is his sermon. He delivers his sermon and hopes that his message gets across to his congregation. The tool man has a blueprint. So does the architect. The corporation accountant has a graph, the chemist a formula, the artist a sketch. The parts are all brought together to achieve a given or desirable end. Each part is subject to analysis and change until it becomes accepted or proved. When understanding of the sermon, the formula and the blueprint occurs, that is when you are ready for action. That is when you become a winner!*

In using words you arrange the ingredients of your formula with the mortar and pestle of knowledge, experience and desire. You have one goal in view—success! By manipulating the ingredients and by adding catalysts you step up the effectiveness of your action. By planning, manipulating and controlling words you guide yourself and your desire into the human orbit where what you are after will become reality.

To help you develop *your* plan-of-action to use words in achieving success, let's call the signals for what they are. Let's use the tools vital to achievement. Let's use that formula *forward-thrust + directional control = Goal.* Let's think of it as the mobile frame upon which to hang the barest essentials of key words and actions that step you up to maximum performance to achieve your goal. Let's weave the magic thread. Let's use the cement that binds the organization of the whole.

The Five Major Tools
Which Play A Role In
The Formula For Success

A number of tools are available to those who would use the power of words as their vehicle to success. These tools are not catalysts. They are methods. They help prepare the present for the future and make things happen. They are the cement binding the organization of your career. These tools may be identified as: 1) the *Directional Map,* 2) your *Time Schedule,* 3) your *Plan-of-Action,* 4) your *Testing Program,* and 5) your *Vehicle for Results.* In brief they are explained as follows:

CONSTRUCTION EQUIPMENT
FOR BUILDING SUCCESS

1. *The directional map*

    To develop your formula for the future, and master your destiny through words, you have to know WHERE you are going. You have to set up goals and the roadway you will follow. You simply have to *know* where you are going. Your guidelines are all such words that indicate "where." They indicate direction and place. *Example:* forward, million-dollar government contract, fleet of taxis, etc. (See Chapter Six and the Kennison Plan!)

2. *The time schedule*

    The time factor deals with the WHEN of your

progress. It pins down the time element so that you can organize to meet the schedule. Such words as "goals," "objectives," "targets," that are part of the *directional map* now become achievement areas tied to a fixed date. You step up production to meet schedule. The goal and the program date become part of the incentive.

3. *The plan-of-action*

You don't know the ball players without a scorecard and you can't get into the game without a working knowledge of how you are going to achieve your goal in a given time. For this purpose you design a *plan-of-action*. You determine the exact program of how you are going to do it. All words you use make you operational toward a given goal in a given time. This central plan should be maintained no matter what handicap or detour may arise.

4. *The testing program*

Here's where you put your ideas out for field testing. No success comes without errors along the way and no successful man has ever been free of failure. To determine what program and what words will be most effective to gain your success, test them on people. Use the same method that manufacturers use in product-testing. Sample an area. See what response you get. If one approach you are making to people with words is meeting a dead end, discard it. Try another approach. Test your approach till you hit on the one that makes your personality stand out. Develop the word-pattern that suits you. Become glib in what you are rehearsing and then go after those goals. Develop your "gift-of-gab."

5. *The vehicle for results*

When you have checked out all your needs for talking your way to success, and have everything programmed for action, you are ready to move up. By such a use of the consruction equipment for building success you have determined your weaknesses, your roadblocks. You have witnessed the end results of each. As a result you correct them. You create a standard. You have five important power tools under control and are ready to make your fortune. You are ready to take the next step now in utilizing communication as the golden energy of success. You are developing the power-thrust to recognition. To the mechanics of all this, add now a dash of imagination.

12

Self-Marketing Strategy Through The "Gift-Of-Gab"

If you have the
"gift-of-gab," and you want
to sell your services into the
bondage of business or
industry, you are a lot like a
company with a new product.
You have to develop it,
field-test it, produce it and
then introduce it to the
common market where it is
most advantageous. You have
to make sharp decisions and
operate fast to cope with
competition.

W here do you start in the matter of self-marketing? You start first with the 4 D's.

The 4 D's That Guide
Self-Marketing Strategy:

1. *Determine* whether there's a need for your talent.
2. *Decide* what industry will be to your advantage.
3. *Design* your route to get there.
4. *Distribute* your talents lavishly until you're in position to gain recognition.

There's a time factor
on personal success

In developing your self-marketing strategy remember that there's a definite time factor involved in achieving success. There's a perishability in your product in the time available to achieve your desires. In your first steps toward success you have a monopoly of which a prospective buyer is yet unaware. You have to make him conscious of your capabilities. You have to ask yourself, How can I determine whether there's a demand for my product? Will what I have to sell click? What price can I set on my services that will put me in an attractive position? How effective will my talents be in a particular industry? Will I be competitive?

If you have facility with words and that gift-of-gab you certainly don't want to be confined to the monotony of a factory production line. You don't want to be stuck on a farm or in a mine. So what do you want to do with that gift-of-gab? Become a radio or television announcer? An evangelistic preacher? A union leader, politician, circus barker, or take a shot at Hollywood? Name it!

FOURTEEN PERSONAL QUESTIONS
TO PIN DOWN SALIENT POINTS

Now ask yourself:

1. *What are my likes and dislikes as I scan the areas where I can fill a need?*
2. *Where would I fit best?*

3. *Who can best use my special talents with words?*
4. *Can I effectively replace someone else with my gift-of-gab?*
5. *Does someone REALLY want my type of talent?*
6. *Will they pay what I think I'm worth?*
7. *Are they in full position to give all my talents full play?*
8. *Am I willing to pay the price of living in a goldfish bowl and wheeling and dealing in Big Time?*
9. *How many possible purchasers of my talent are there?*
10. *Is my gift-of-gab just right for them?*
11. *Can I improve for their benefit as well as for mine?*
12. *Am I better than the existing talent they already have?*
13. *Will I continue to produce effectively?*
14. *Will I stand up under pressure?*

**Inventory your answers
and go into action!**

With your personal replies to these questions in mind, deliberately make a decision—and here's how to do it:

*Four Key Moves
in Self-Marketing:*

1. *Determine what you do best!*
2. *Pinpoint the industry* that most needs your service!
3. *Determine who will pay high* for your gift-of-gab.
4. *Map out the program* for how you will educate your future employer about your talents.

**Let's use a real
live example now**

Let's say it's *you!* Let's say that when you were in high school you found yourself possessed of a smooth capacity to "talk." You found it easy to persuade people. Then you matriculated in the university. In the department of speech you took courses in radio, television, dramatics, etc. In the natural course of events, due to your gift-of-gab, you won local, state and regional recognition in "public speaking" and declamation. Somehow you had the *"feel"* of an audience. You knew instinctively that you could sway an audience with words, that you could play persuasively and increasingly well on public emotion. Yet your love was not for "declamation" or oratory. Your real love wasn't in the hundreds of roles you played for Theatre-in-the-Round or on the Straw Hat Circuit, or in writing, directing and producing shows on the university's radio and TV stations.

In the spring you attended the senior interviews where the "bird dogs" of industry sniff out the kind of talent they like to feed in to the corporate system.

But you don't like the cloistered grind of the pyramid-climbers. You want creative expression without repression or restriction. You don't want to be tied down in a groove in which the status seekers glide to executive class.

So one day you're producing a fraternity house playlet in honor of the retiring house mother. It's a take-off on the current television show called *"This Is Your Life"* and suddenly you know what you want to do. You want to do interview-type shows on TV. You can be with people. With your fertile imagination you can come up with human interest angles even as you show off your talents.

In the television business you don't want to start "cold," so after graduation from the university you farm out at a small TV station. Here you learn that the commercial outlet is a little more rugged than at college. But it's no obstacle. You're still moving along smoothly as you do everything from being the station's sulky race reporter at the county fair to acting as merchandising manager. Then you query a bigger television station. You go from a Midwest 5,000-watter to a 50,000-watter. Here you find fertile new areas in your specialized field. You gain local popularity, and your fame is spreading. You're still eyeing New York, Chicago, and the Sunset Slot in Hollywood.

In the meantime accumulated experience is distilling and redistilling ideas for an audience or talent-participation show. You write half-a-dozen pilot scripts. In the privacy of your bedroom you enact the role you'll play as master of ceremonies on a golden giveaway show. You type out a program presentation and put it in a beautiful jacket, buy yourself an attaché case and an airline ticket to New York. You're off! You've decided to bypass NBC and CBS for a crack at the lustrous meccas on Madison Avenue, the glory-founts of creativity, the lane of lucre for the talent that makes it.

Here the advertising agencies are hives of excitement. Nobody at Benton and Bowles has time to listen to you. They're too excited about their new computer system. Batten, Barton, Durstine and Osborne turn you down. A sharp little vice president one block away, however, sees you as a great talent for a Quinn Martin Production and he lights up like a pinball machine as he hears you out.

From here on in you are public property. You live the goldfish bowl way of life and green makes fertile mountains in your bankbook. You do movie shorts in your spare hour. Then along comes a night show and more golden bucks plop in your coffers. Your fortune is made. You've finally found your niche and to get all this all it took was (a) determining where the need was for your talent, (b) deciding what industry could best serve you, (c) designing the route to get there, and then (d) distributing your talents to create a national image and become the success you desire. YOU HAVE TALKED YOUR WAY TO SUCCESS!

This is just one experience of many in one of many fields. It is one of many avenues of expression which a young man with a gift-of-gab can follow if he has the guts to keep at it even when the world seems to fall in. This example is cited only to point out the process marked from producer of the talent to the consumer. The process is that of entrepreneurs who have unabashedly stepped into the future on their face value . . . and then, through the dramatic power of words and action, fooled everyone by becoming a hit!

You too can be a success!

You too can come up with a personal marketing concept . . . and be a hit! You too can meet the increasing challenge of today and deliver what the consumer wants to buy. Like a company with a new product you have to introduce yourself. You have to use self-marketing strategy to produce a payoff on the route to the Golden Bonuses.

THREE CONTRA-INDICATIONS IN
VOCAL CONTACT WITH PEOPLE

1. Never speak deprecatingly of yourself!

Within you are the basic essentials that you need for success, so why run yourself down? Why tear your soul apart stewing over a few personal weak links? Why take the starch out of the high collar of your pride? Why weaken your backbone through self-disapproval? In turn, why use this method as an indirect way to ask for sympathy! Self-depreciation is a saboteur to pride. It's the negative approach when a positive stand serves you better. It lowers the boom on morale. Therefore, in your design for living give yourself the Big Build-up. Do it as follows:

Self-incentives for
Stepping up Your Go-Power!

1. *Raise your sights and goals.*
2. *Elevate your self-estimation.*
3. *Picture yourself in the top role.*
4. *Think only in terms of your assets.*
5. *Meet all emergencies head-on.*
6. *Walk up to opportunity and take it by the hand.*
7. *Act, walk, talk like you've always been a champion!*

It's all right to be conscious of your handicaps. It's good to know your deficits. But let them lie. Don't dwell on them. Remember, you absolutely have all the ingredients you need for success. You have the same cubic centimeter-sized brain as those who are already successful, so use it! *NEVER run yourself down!*

2. Don't be concerned with details

Concern with details in ordinary conversation has no place. In affairs-of-state and intricate matters details are of course necessary. But in normal business or social conversation avoid consuming your time or anyone else's time with unnecessary details. Details in conversation mean loss of productive time when there are so many other methods of getting the same message across. Details are unnecessary detours. They are interference with a normal course of action. For this reason I believe that wherever it is possible, assign details to someone who prefers to work in details. Keep your mind free to think big! At the beginning of your career this may not be possible. You may have to handle details to acquire self-discipline and control. But! You DON'T have to handle them through conversation! Put them in writing! Then no one forgets.

3. Avoid all possible betraying statements

Thinking is stimulated by prodding the sensory organs. Sight, hearing and touch are identified and interpreted to cause you to exclaim when a circumstance is not right. Under adverse circumstances, in anger or fear, you may cry out and the language you use can lower someone's estimate of you. Guard yourself against such exclamations. Build a wall over your emotions. Don't let emotions or sensitivities show.

Here's What You Gain by
Avoiding Vocal Contra-indications:

- *You maintain self-confidence* by telling the world that you are the greatest!

- *You displace talk with action.* You avoid the anchors of inconseqential conversation.

- *You maintain self-respect* through you own personality build up. As you develop your *Impression Circle* you develop your *Personality Appeal.*

Self-rest and self-confidence are vital to your plan-of-action. They are vital to self-preservation. If you have something to say, say it distinctly. Speak constructively only. Speak only when what you have to say adds weight to what has alrady been said. If you have nothing to say, make it a point to shut your mouth!

In developing the positive approach to talking your way to success it is also necessary to learn when to listen. On this score I suggest that you—

Expand your thinking
through listening

Knowing what the other person is thinking is the secret to most product-merchandising success. Knowing what others believe to be their needs shapes your thinking to supply them. For this reason *it becomes necessary to feel the pulse of popular thinking and you can do this simply by listening.*

The art of listening is an art that has to be developed. Listening is vital to the person who would expand his thinking by way of his ears. Listening is vital to hearing the inner voice of your own thinking as new ideas stimulate your brain and your wants into more effective channels. To tune up your ears for listening leading to BIG thinking, here are some suggested methods:

Six Techniques for Triggering Creative Thoughts:

1. Ask questions
2. Ask advice
3. Ask for ideas
4. Ask for facts
5. Ask for help
6. Ask . . . and THEN LISTEN!

There are certain salient assets to asking questions. They not only elicit information but draw others to you. Your questions give people a chance to have THEIR say. Asking questions makes friends, so *ask questions with intent to listen!* Ask questions with intent to profit! Ask questions with the intent to make your own personal wants pay off in Golden Goals as you talk your way to success! Make decisions on that score *now!*

Decision-Making Vital
In Self-Marketing

The act of "making up your mind" is one of the beginnings of success. "Making up your mind" is called *decision.*

Decision is mental organization

Decision coordinates and correlates your problems. It dissolves confusion and puts orderliness in your habits, feelings and behavior.

It gets everything under control and the direct result of it all is the lessening of personal tension. Feelings of inadequacy melt. Stress dissolves. Euphoria takes over.

If you would make decisions, get off of the fence! *Stop being neutral!* Stop conforming! Accept challenges! Walk right up to a challenge and grab it by the hair! Stop doubting! Get in there and talk your way up to your goals. Believe in yourself. Respect yourself, your goals and your competitors. When you hit obstacles, bounce off and start again. MOVE into the future with deliberate decision and desire.

Nicki Manetti had to make up *her* mind. Nicki was a concert pianist. For the many years that I knew her as a patient she refused to marry because she said she had to take care of her invalid mother. Then her mother died. Nicki married. She married a cripple. Once again her career was anchored and her booking agent was irate. He wanted to know why she had hopped from the frying pan into the fire, and Nicki couldn't answer his question . . . not at the time.

Then Nicki began to realize that she was living a new kind of hell, a new kind of frustration, a new kind of disaster area that was slowly eating away the time factor in her personal success.

One day she showed up at my office all battered and hurt. Her husband had beaten her with his cane. As I bandaged her lesions her crying suddenly stopped. I looked up. There was cold resolve on her face as she made a decision.

She said she was tired of letting others lean on her, that she wanted her freedom, that she wanted to pursue her career. She wanted to take her beautiful talent to the world and this is exactly what she did.

Not too long ago Nicki returned from a long successful European tour. She'd even made it big in Russia, and she was happy with her success. She received her divorce and today her mind's at ease. The decision she made paid off!

Decisions cause fear to leave

The moment you make up your mind you will find that your fears will dissipate. Open your mind and you will find that there is no necessity to hesitate or haggle, no need to fret. You will come awake and your life will take on new meaning, new fullness, new direction! As the result of decision new powers will develop within yourself and all of this can be diverted into channels productive to reaching and maintaining a career.

How to handle the problems of decision

No one becomes a success without having had to make decisions, decisions which are all in the form of words. Success is intimately related to decision-making and the following factors must be kept constantly in mind:

At all times:

1. *Make no "snap decisions"*

   Investigate first. Act second. Snap judgments too often are completely wrong.

2. *Once a decision is made stick to it*

   Never change horses in the middle of the stream unless the one you're on is dead. If the situation warrants, change horses fast.

3. *Remember that other people are also influenced*

   Every decision you make also influences someone else around you, so make those decisions profitable in your move toward success.

4. *Be well informed before deciding on anything*

   Never jeopardize your possibilities for success by making decisions that will put you in a negative position. Once you are in a bad light you are anchored to mediocrity. Anyone in the camera eye will soon tell you that bad lighting can quickly kill a career.

Decision-making is a lonely business

Like a boxer, an aerialist, a gymnast, a concert pianist, or a fighter pilot, when you are reaching for success you suddenly become aware that you are very much alone. By yourself you have to win or lose on the basis of the decisions in your performance.

Decisions don't come easy. They come by repetition and work. The more decisions you make the better becomes your performance and the more confident and competent becomes your performance. In stepping up to success you have to learn to adjust to the lonely business of taking the stairsteps alone. In stepping up to success learn to count more upon yourself and less upon others. Become as self-sufficient as possible. Be willing to take on more responsibility. Be willing to make decisions that indicate your broadening capability for sharing a load.

Don't waste time when making decisions

Decision-making is often put off. Because someone can't come to a decision, a career may be lost. Businesses, large and small, have been lost because of the failure to make a decision. Lack of decision is costly, so if you would achieve success make your decisions sharp and clear no matter what the cost. Put those decisions prominently into words! Define them!

Wence Markley made a decision. Wence was a physician friend of mind who dabbled in real estate investments. He bought a pair of apartment houses and went deeply into debt. Then a shopping center deal presented itself and the lure was strong. Profit was 16 per cent on the possible investment. All the words spelled out a terrific gain. Should he trade the apartment houses, sell his house, borrow on his insurance or let the opportunity slide by? It was a delectable deal and Wence's mouth watered for it. He neglected his practice worrying about it. With such an investment property he protested that he could retire early and live high. Then Wence began to ask himself questions. The words all came out one way. They pointed up that Wence just wasn't a businessman. He wouldn't know what to do with a shopping center if he had one. He was a doctor and if he wanted to dabble in investments it had to be as a hobby and that was all. The decision made Wence return to his practice once more. Now he has peace of mind. His patients are having peace of body as well, and he's making a lot more money than ten per cent on an investment.

In your self-marketing strategy *decision-making* is absolutely necessary to prevent being chopped down in the competitive tree. It's vital to remember those 4 D's—that you *determine* whether there is a need for your talent, that you *decide* in what industry you will show to your best advantage, that you *design* your personal program for self-promotion and that you *distribute* your talents lavishly until you're in a position for recognition.

Once the decision is made, start the ball rolling! Use that *gift-of-gab*. Talk up a storm. If someone tends to steal your thunder, brew up another storm. When the storm's over and the sun comes out, make hay of the grass that is growing under the other fellow's feet. Like my grandfather used to say, "The dictionary is the only place where you will find success before work."

I liked my balding grandfather. I wanted to be just like him. I not only wanted to talk like him but to look like him, and one day it came to a head when we went into the barbershop. I got into the chair and the barber looked me over.

"How'd you like it cut, kid?"

"Like Gramp's."

"How's that?"

"Short, with a hole on top."

There you have the power of words. There's the decision. It's self-marketing and you're the one who has to make the choice. You're the one who has to put it into words. You are the one who has to sell other people on your wants. You have to determine, decide, design and distribute your talents until you're in position to receive recognition. From there on in you're top man. The decisions are yours. So are the words that make you famous . . . and all it takes is learning the art of letting yourself *glow!*

13

Do You Feel A Song Coming On?

In *using words as a vehicle to success, get on the bandwagon of vivacious terminology and be exciting to be near. Be excited about living. Be excited about everything around you. Use the magnetic pull of words to draw people into your magic circle of Personality Appeal. Fit the right words to the right music and for the rest of your life you'll feel a song coming on!*

"The moment I feel a wave of depression, or negative thinking, coming on," explains tiny Mabs Tiernan, "I say to myself, *'I feel a song coming on'* and it gives me a psychological lift."

Mabs is a tiny mite, a delightful adult moppet subject to the pressures of her profession. She's an interior designer for famous RIKE'S of Dayton, Ohio, and the pressures get to her. In selling her products and her ideas she has to be "turned on" and tuned to the positive. She can't afford to lose self-control with clients.

To maintain her enthusiasm and high spirits she indoctrinates herself each morning with positive thinking. She tells herself it's a great morning, a great day. She turns it on mentally and soon her body is tuned to the same wave length.

"When I do this," she explains, "I'm no longer depressed. I feel happy and successful and full of energy. Call it what you want but when I say to myself *'I feel a song coming on'* that's my approach to peace of mind and body.

"When I say this to myself I get an ego lift as well as physical refueling. More than that, I feel that it creates personal attractiveness and I do better at my work. Positive attracts positive. NOT negative! It also attracts an elevated income and this is ultimately the measure of success, Yes indeed, I feel a song coming on!"

Develop enthusiasm in daily living

According to Mabs ENTHUSIASM is an invigorating aura of charm that surrounds the vivacious person with a powerful and contagious attraction. It literally draws people to you so *turn it on!* Create the personality pull that makes others succumb to what you have to say. Develop this thing called *Personality Appeal.*

Believe in yourself! Believe in what you have to say and make it ring. Be interested in people enough to make this interest show. Express it! Use colorful terminology that packs an electrically charged message. Use words that hold exhilarating self-sufficiency. Use words that blush with vitality. Use words of color to get what you want out of life.

Psychologist Vince Black of Professional Research says: "Use the forward-thrust of words with defined objectives, guided direction and thoughtful control. Use them enthusiastically, colorfully and with purpose! Let their exuberance demonstrate your enthusiasm as well as your faith in yourself. Let words demonstrate your self-confidence, self-reliance and personal effectiveness in your job or profession. Use them with the completely selfish desire to win friends and influence people through personal charm. Use them to talk your way to success with people!

Establish contact through
devices at your command

Four Major Steps
For Getting Through To People

Step One

Enthusiasm

If you are not getting through to people—if the face or faces before you remain blank—then *turn on your enthusiasm!* Be dramatic! Touch on your listener's sensitivity areas. Touch those magic buttons of his wants and make him come alive with interest in what you have to say.

You will not only feel the result of your persuasion on people. You will feel it as well. The moment you walk across that bridge of words into the lives of people you will have created *directional control*. You will have established rapport.

Make a precise effort to reach into people's minds if you would talk your way to success. Step up the *forward-thrust* of the words you use. I repeat, let people know that you understand their wants, their desires, their viewpoints. Let them know that you like them and that you have a sympathetic understanding of their needs. Be enthusiastic in doing it and you will get through to people every time.

Step Two

Visual Aids

Maybe you are no Cicero or Demosthenes, no William Jennings Bryan or Clarence Darrow, but you can still use the tricks of their trade. Use visual gimmicks to supplement your oral argument.

Add another gun to your armament. Tie your charts, your displays, your chalk-talks in with his wants. What does he want: security, a job, food, clothing, peace of mind? Then try to answer his wants. He needs it! He listens to you and watches you, hoping that you have the key to answering his problems. He is already hoping you can fill his need.

Step Three

TAKE ACTION

Make your listeners *want* to take action. Tell them they have something to gain from what you have to say or sell. Appeal to their sense of values and sense of reason as well. Appeal to that which they want most. Deliberately outline the benefits they will get. Let them see how they will profit, how they can get satisfaction and pleasure, how they will achieve distinction and be satisfied. Help them step up their self-respect and personal pride. Maintain their dignity and hand-feed the right words into them just as deliberately as a surgeon prepares a surgical field. Get your listener receptive and the moment he is receptive he will act under your *directional control*. Through the living force of words you will have created a rudder to divert his life.

Step Four

PLAY IT SMART

Anyone can flip a switch to turn on an electric light but it takes more than a flip to turn people on. To get the support of people, to get their cooperation, to talk your way to sucess, you have to inspire and maintain action. You have to get the listener to move in the direction requested. How persuasively you activate your audience determines how successfully you get through to it. It depends on eliciting interest, stepping up wants and getting a response, and this is playing it smart. Every time you open your mouth to speak you are a salesman. The "pitch" is on. The "sell" begins the moment another person comes into view, or you go out on a stage. He's your prospect, so express interest in him. Once he picks up your interest in him he will come your way. That's when you play it smart and tell him what to do. You've used the social color of words to influence him.

The Social Color Of Words
And How They Brighten Your Life
To Lower Your Tensions

A symphony of sight and sound is painted in the leashed power of hues and shades and shadows that influence human lives from day to day. A symphony of these same colors is packed in the power of words. In the sight and sound of words is success!

Color, in this symphony of sight and sound, can be used to reduce tensions as well as carry a message. Color, in words, may play a vibrant role in day-to-day living. Words cannot be erased. They cannot be shut out. They cannot be turned off permanently because the emotional representations of the color in words cannot be rejected except by those who have a mental block, an emotional inhibition, are deaf, or have ears that are color-blind.

Mental distress such as moodiness and nervousness may begin with negative words, the wrong words. For this reason color in words should be considered a cause, as well as a release, for tension on the job. Because it is an influence on our daily lives we should recognize the colors in words for what they are. We should know them and then use them for what they are!

What is color in words?

Color in words is a wave length of energy. It is charm and hate, kindness and anger, and in relationship to its place on the vocal spectrum and as an influence on the human mind, color in words is a stimulant, a depressant, an irritant or sedative. It is many things to many people as they use words to match and mismatch their personalities and temperaments. In their lack of knowledge about the power of words they contribute to their own tension.

Color in words may inspire happiness. It may inspire gloom. It can frighten people, confuse or blind them. It can arouse interest or shriek out in agony. It can steal from a person, as was so neatly done by El Greco. On his sumptuous canvases the artist wrapped splendorous clothing around sallow-faced decadents. He actually lost the people in the dramatics of color.

The senses of smell, taste, touch, hearing and sight work together. Since color influences sight and sound, it plays a starring role in emotional stability. The nervous system is affected. For this reason color in words should be kept harnessed to relieve tension rather than aggravate it day after day.

Harness color and
you harness power

Color in words commands attention. It creates interest and inspires desire. It can be used to set you up for action or lower your morale. Because of this influence it can also be used to lower your tension level even as you manipulate words to achieve goals of success.

Harness the color in words as you harness decorator's colors in fabric and paint. Create an environment of warmth: the warmth of your personality. Utilize the gay shades of yellow and red. Add touches of blue and utilize "cold color" accents to make the warmer colors more vivacious. This is the contrast and comparison, the change of pace, the hot and the cold of emotions.

Carefully harnessed, color in words can be used to give a psychological lift to get rid of moodiness and depression. Because of the necessity for the careful harnessing of this power color in words must be used in the right place at the right time, in the right shade, on the right people!

Know colorful words! Know the adjectives, the adverbs and the bright nouns. Know their uses and when to use them. Remember that perception depends on association. *If you are associated with dull colorless words people will think of you as a dull person.* Because of this you must THINK in terms of colorful words. Act with colorful words. Use words to create harmony and unity. Use them to give variety and movement to your daily life. Use them to establish and step up your *Personality Appeal* as well as to relieve tension.

How Tranquilizer Pills
Effectively Kill Words And The Success-Drive

Stress and strain build nervous tension. One daily crisis after another contributes to the feeling of being at high pitch and this is exactly where you are on the success-route. You ARE at high pitch when you start moving up the scale toward the Golden Goals and that's the way it should be. This is Nature's way of adapting your body to the desires of your mind.

Are pills the passport
to tension release?

Those who dose themselves on tranquilizers are actually depriving themselves of the very natural power they need to get ahead. They lose their fighting edge. They lose capacity to adapt to new situations. They lose the *forward thrust* that comes with a physiology primed by fear and excitement and the necessity for self-preservation as well as self-awareness. They kill the mind's capability to be brilliant. They anesthetize the brain's ability to produce words. *Pills are NO passport to tension release.* In fact, tranquilizer pills can assassinate goal-getting power. They can effectively close off that award-winning word supply.

Tranquilizers are a
hindrance to progress

Man does not live by bread alone and he does not live by alien chemistry that slows him down. He cannot escape from anxiety and stress through pills if he is shooting for the top. Pills ARE a hindrance to his progress. They are not the passport to tension release. Instead they are a childish failure to face up to fact. They simply draw the shades on the face of trouble, and opposition, and conquest, in a direct admission of weakness and inability to face the problem for what it is.

**You have to face up
to facts to survive**

There is no escape from actuality. If you've got problems to meet, face up to them. Use the physiological power that Nature gives you during stress and the flight to success. Use the outlet of words. Use the drive that is normal in "tension." Expand that power fruitfully rather then let it convert your stomach and bowels into a no-man's-land of ulcers, spastic colon and other neurotic behavior.

Tensions are normal. Fears are normal until YOU make them abnormal. There's anxiety in everything you do and when your wants aren't immediately filled you're temporarily frustrated. Escaping from frustration through the veil of drugs is the last thing to do. It's simply no answer to achieving success. In fact, it's a detriment. It helps no one but the drug industry.

> *There's a time and a place for drugs but there's no place for the synthetic "bliss" that comes from mood pills. Money doesn't buy freedom from fact, yet $100 million is spent by Americans yearly on tranquilizers to lay the groundwork for their own defeat. Tranquilizers hinder progress! They effectively kill the success drive! They not only stop off the success drive but neutralize the best tranquilizer you'll ever have . . . WORDS!*

How To Be Sharp About
Flat Emotional Notes

Anger:

A person who is wrong seldom admits it. The person who is wrong is usually angry and anger is the wind that blows out the light of the mind. So why spend time being angry? Why complain? Why not become completely self-aware of your emotional trigger areas and wash them away. Delete words of anger from your mind and from your voice at all times.

Instead of complaining, DO SOMETHING! Leaders never make an issue of hardship. The pioneers of this nation overcame unbelievable odds. They fought everything there was to fight and came through even when food, water, horses, equipment and families were wiped out. They spent very little time with the words of complaint. They were too busy creating. They simply had no time to use words of complaint. This is also true on the frontiers of today.

Dissatisfaction:

Blessed are they who are not satisfied to let well enough alone. All the advances of the world as we know them came from those who were dissatisfied. They became successes achieving that which they didn't have. They probed with words and actions until they achieved change.

Indifference:

"There is something very particularly harmful about indifference," said a Minneapolis clergyman. "Indifference is not only harmful— it is dangerous. It weakens every enterprise. It stifles every venture the soul makes and disrupts every relationship which might otherwise have been beautiful. Indifference can be deadly."

Worry:

The Anglo-Saxon word "worry" originally meant to choke oneself. Therefore why choke off success? Why kill your future by worrying? Mark Twain said, "I am an old man and have known many troubles but most of them never happened."

Worry takes up as much time as does work and work pays better dividends, so why not work instead of worry? Why let worry pull tomorrow's clouds over today's sunshine? Become aware of what it is and why it exists. Then eliminate it! Erase the words of worry from your mind. Use the forward motion of bright cheerful words and watch your own emotions change. Use the *forward-thrust* of colorful words that brighten everyone's day.

Doubts, fears and hate:

Ralph Waldo Emerson, the American essayist, said: "Don't waste your life in doubts and fears. Spend yourself on the work before you, well assured that the right performance of this hour's duty will be the best preparation for the hours or ages that follow it." Harry Emerson Fosdick said, "Hating people is like burning down your house to get rid of a rat." So be aware of the better approach. Get rid of your abnormal tensions. Get rid of the negative words that stimulate them.

We are placed in a structure of reality called environment. How we respond to what is around us depends on how much we care about achieving success. It depends on emotional motivation and self-awareness. It depends on the degree of anxiety that "bugs" us. It depends on the words we use to think up to happiness and success that bring us peace of mind.

It has been said that "mental health" is a state of being without anxiety but this is not true. There's a degree of normal anxiety, just like there's a degree of normal tension, in all success. Anxiety exists because of the responsibilities that go with success and this is a fundamental fragment of our life.

For those who would think big and go on to success there has to be a realization that there is a difference between normal anxiety and neurotic anxiety and we cannot run away from any kind of anxiety without sacrificing some kind of freedom. We cannot run away from the influence of words used to stimulate these anxieties. We have to roll with the punches, accept them, and then move on.

We grow into freedom and into success by accepting responsibilities. With these responsibilites come varied types of anxieties. In these anxieties the thinking man turns to something stronger than himself. He turns to God and the proof that there IS a God is that you and I need him. He turns to God with words called "prayer."

You are never alone

The successful person who uses the words of prayer finds that God is always at his elbow. In prayer he finds strength. In prayer, and the words of prayer, you may come upon love and belief and faith. In prayer you may find the words that suddenly make you conscious of your own internal strength as you reach out for help, as you reach out for confidence, as you reach out for succor.

When you hit the bumps on the road to success try turning to God. Turn to the source of goodness. Use the words of prayer that give you solace, words that make you happier and more content. Gather strength through meditation.

In your prayers use simple words, direct words, and say thanks. Make no requests. Don't tell God what to do. He already knows your problems. He'll help when you need it. Help will come even when you don't need it because He guides your subconscious mind. From this amazing segment of the brain will come the ways and means for reaching success. From this magic source will come the power-thrust you need. From it all will come the *directional control.* So why not talk with God?

Why not find spiritual strength in the midst of confusion? Why not use words of prayer to bring you calm? Why not solve problems by sharing with God those words that bring your problems into focus? Why not solve emotional stress in a manner that drugs and psychotherapy can never touch?

Develop faith in yourself that you will be a success! Develop belief! Develop honesty and sincerity and work at it and your prayers will be answered.

Whether you are a check-out clerk at a supermarket or an executive in a big plant, the necessity is to use words as a vehicle to success. The necessity is to develop the condition of mind that becomes enthusiastic with the goals ahead, a condition of mind that is like a firecracker waiting for the fuse to be lit so that the action of success can begin.

14

How To Press The Right Buttons In Public Imagination

Stand up to be counted . . .
Speak up to be recognized . . .
Be able to motivate others if
you would be a winner. Use
words as the lifeblood of
talking your way to success
with people. Use words to
press the right buttons in
public imagination if you
would be a winner. Use words
efficiently in an age when
success depends on one's
personal ability to persuade.

Press The Buttons
Of The Trigger Zones

T ouch people where they are tender if you would have them be moved. Do it with words that have dramatic descriptive power. Give them the picture you would paint and hit them between the eyes with the kind of terminology they understand. Touch on what they sense and what they feel. Press the buttons of the seven senses of mankind.

V. A. Ketcham calls these senses the *"Seven Doors to the Mind"* and you can enter these doorways at will if you try. How? Give people something they can see, something they can feel. In the descriptive power of words make them smell, make them taste, make them experience hot and cold and sense of touch. When you create the word pictures that press these buttons you are "getting through." You are touching the buttons of public imagination and this is the way to talk your way to success with people!

All people are picture- or word-minded so give them words that inspire mental pictures. Unlimber your descriptive genius. Tell a fast-moving story. Make every word count. Here now are some examples:

The Seven Senses
To Touch In Speech-Making

O D O R—(sense of smell)
Example of word-usage:

"Death pushed at me as I stepped into the barren blight of Buchenwald. The odor of burning flesh was strong."

S I G H T
Example:

"The front of the Chinese Embassy at Saigon bulged and burst as the Viet Cong bomb went off. Through the gaping hole vomited people and property. The massive hole was a doorway to death."

HEARING
Example:

"Night-born crickets scratched the body of darkness with a rasping note. It was an unending note that I could hear just dimly as the anesthesia of sleep came on."

TASTE
Example:

"I bit into that thick succulent steak and all heaven came out."

TACTILE—(sense of feel)
Example:

"To start with, Mike's face was a rugged mountain of tortured flesh. His cheeks, nose, brow, and jaw were a jumble of rocky abutments tossed crazily into position by a cataclysm called heredity and he couldn't run away from it. After ten years of the second and third rate prize-ring circuits it was even worse. After his last fight they brought him into my office. As my fingers ran over his face I could feel the disaster of scar tissue around his eyes, the nose I'd re-set a dozen times, the ears that were gnarled and thick, and like every time before, I got sick inside."

MOTOR—(sense of movement)
Example:

"The car slid around the corner and its wheels screamed. The automobile careened and twisted like an epileptic having fits. It hit a fire hydrant, rolled, and came to a crunching halt against the wall."

THERMIC—(sense of temperature)
Example:

"The tropic heat of Acapulco pushed in on me as if it were a surging wall of flame. I no longer sweated. I felt sick. I puked all over the bananas."

In other words USE WORDS THAT TELL THE STORY! Make them graphic! Use words that picture what you have to say! In picturing what you have to say, here are some very intimate tricks-of-the-trade used by master public speakers. Here are eleven hot tips on what you can do as you master the art of pressing the right buttons of public imagination.

PERSONAL TIPS FOR ELECTRIFYING THOSE WHO HEAR

√ *Make sincerity ring out!*

Nothing grabs an audience so fast as does frankness and the feeling of honest explanation. So don't just say it! Portray it! Use those "seven doorways"! Make people feel! Make them believe! Make every statement vibrant with the vitality of your message. If you have something to say, SAY it! Say it plainly! Create receptivity by fertilizing the soil of imagination before you plant the seed. Set the mood with your sincerity. Then drive the point home.

Be genuine and believable if you would get through to people and press the right buttons in their imagination. If you would have others understanding you, you have to understand the impact of the sounds that you make. You have to be able to stimulate this impact. "Speaker of the Year" Kenneth McFarland puts it this way, "Effective speech must be an outpouring of one's own convictions, ideals, experience, knowledge and faith."*

√ *Be intimate*

Make what you have to say reach out and kiss the listeners. Radiate your message to them. Into the consonants, vowels and resonance or your discourse pack the intimacy of your million-dollar personality and you will no longer sound dull. People will not see or hear you as being dull. In their eyes you will be attractive.

√ *Be effective without affectation*

How you deliver words to an audience makes you attractive or distractive. To reap the grand benefits of success you have to not

---

* Kenneth McFarland, *Eloquence in Public Speaking* (Englewood Cliffs, N.J.: Prentice-Hall, Inc., 1961), p. 50.

just appear unaffected but *you have to be different!* This means getting through to people via attractive and convincing means. To be effective vocally talk easily, conversationally, be natural. Don't strain at it even as you punch your message across. Exaggerate a little, of course, but at all times be "natural" in doing it.

√ *Put the message across*

No statement goes by without some element of showmanship being involved to distinguish it. Inflections, innuendo, even the replacement of a word with a glance tells a story. Use your voice and your words as mobile units to make you appear different from other people. Develop distinctive notes and be consistent with them. Use terminology that fits your character.

√ *Maintain the "alive-look"*

The most beautiful music dies with a poor musician. Beautiful words die in the mouths of those without flame or passion. From the lips of a vital person words can come alive! They can become vivacious and persuasive! It's up to you to develop that "Alive-Look"! Show that vitality which mesmerizes others into action just like your own. Give them the selling pitch and get them thinking your way.

√ *Show poise and authority*

When you speak, *speak* with confidence. *Show* confidence! Play the role! Be so thoroughly trained in the use of your voice and body that both become persuasive vehicles for your message. This *feel of authority* can come only with rehearsal and constant repetition. It comes only with constant use. Your competence and effectiveness as a speaker are in direct proportion to what you have practiced and learned. Your poise and your authority depend on your demonstrations of power.

√ *Say it pleasingly, clean and clear*

Words take pronunciation. They take enunciation and clarity of diction. They take opening your mouth to say them, so get rid of that letter-slot mouth. Deliver! Punch your point across plainly, clearly, pleasingly and with style. Words are your vehicle to fame.

√ *Don't be afraid of emotions! Portray them! Arouse mood!*

No matter what your subject may be—even the dullest event in history—you have to rouse emotion and mood. Stimulate laughter, passion, charity, romance, invention, pleasure, or tears. Develop your voice and the words that sell what you have to sell. Once you learn the gracious act of persuasion, learn to *turn it on and off at will!* Success comes only through persistence, so learn to persuade people through the magic of words. Develop words as the throughway to the minds of men.

√ *Give your words a natural flow*

To be appealing to the eye and ear, words should have a natural flow. The spoken words may be dreamy, pounding, sharp, precise, machined or as polished as you make them. Words should be marked by punctuation, pauses and inflections as they move along. The sentence structure you create should fit the tempo of the message you are putting across or the emotion you would portray. In excitement, sentences are short, clipped. Short phrases are dramatic. Punch lines are exciting, inflammatory. Long phrases are soothing, relaxing, and are designed to create calm. In developing the mood of your pitch, build to a climax. *Then DRIVE your point home!*

√ *Develop change-of-pace*

If you would not just woo your listeners and effectively persuade them, pull the stops on using methods that influence people to your way of thinking. Step up or down to new levels. Change pace. Change tempo. Lag a little in dramatic places. Camouflage the underlying dramatization but still punch the point across. "Schmaltz it up" and give each word, each phrase, "the treatment."

√ *Put the emphasis where it counts*

Never emphasize insignificant words. Never stress two words in succession such as "BIG FOG." Some words tie phrases together. Words like "for," "the," "and," "in the," "don't you," "could have been," etc. are all necessary but DO NOT STRESS THEM. Being overly dramatic on secondary words kills the listener's ear, so put the emphasis where it counts. Use words where they help you most! Put the emphasis on words to win and don't forget for one moment that we are living in an age where success depends on the ability to persuade.

Stand up now and be counted

Before taking the next step to voice improvement let's return a moment to Chapter 2 and the *"self-awareness"* chart. Cover the answer column with a sheet of paper. Then re-answer the questions. On completion withdraw the cover sheet to the right. Compare your answers. Note how in most part many of your answers have changed. Note your new comprehension of words and of yourself as you stand up to be counted. Now is the time to ask yourself some new questions. These are intimate questions, questions that are very personal as you think in terms of talking your way to success with people.

SELF-RATING SCALE

Ask yourself: Yes No

1. Am I penetrating public imagination?   ....
2. Is my opinion being respected?   ....
3. Does what I have to say contribute to my
   success?   ....
4. Am I beginning to speak up when I have
   something to say?   ....
5. Have I developed a philosophy of life to
   carry others along?   ....
6. Does what I have to say carry a message?   ....
7. Are my words freighted with punch?   ....
8. Do I speak with authority?   ....
9. Do I develop in people a desire for action?   ....
10. Am I commanding attention?   ....
11. Am I convincing?   ....
12. Am I sincere?   ....
13. Am I appealing to human dignity?   ....
14. Am I beginning to know how to press the
    right buttons in public imagination?   ....

> NOTE: *If the majority of your answers are positive, and you have already outgrown that original self-awareness chart, then you are getting through. You are beginning to utilize the basic fundamentals in talking your way to success.*

Carry this self-rating scale a bit further. Is there something about my voice that gives me a hard time in getting through to people? Do they sense the tenseness in my vocal tones? Does my voice quaver, waver or vibrate? Does it give the impression of uncertainty, insincerity or unwillingness? Does it portray what I want to say or does it render a misconception? What do people actually hear when they close their eyes and listen to me? Does this process change their concept of me? Has my voice sufficient personality and character to sustain what I have to say?

If you have answered most of these questions positively let's move ahead. Let's advance into methods and procedures now as we consider the voice itself.

Your Voice And Its
Contribution To Persuasion

Let's start from scratch: Do people like to listen to you? Do you make what you have to say palatable? Is what you say understandable or are you bombing your listeners into apathy? Do you have bad linguistic habits or mannerisms?

> *In using your voice, and your words, as a through-way to success, remember that it is not your classic tones but how well you use those tones to manipulate mood and thought in the listener. It is in how you arouse that listener to action to achieve what you want most of all.*

Intimate tricks
in the vocal department

Words, and the music of words, remain ineffective until such time as you learn to convert them into living portraits.

To help you develop your use of words, here are some tricks-of-the-trade used by show-business people. Each is a part of the other, and if you would be a winner all these tricks have to be woven one into the other as you talk your way to success.

How to Improve Your Voice

1. *Relax!*

   When your tensions release you can deliver your message with complete freedom. Let go!

2. *Breathe naturally*

   Keep your lungs full and your sentences "air full" to the end. "Breathe from the belly." Don't suck your abdomen in when your diaphragm pushes up into your lungs. Make it push out instead.

3. *Get your voice across the front row*

   Project, or throw, your voice over the footlights. Get through to everyone. Hit the people in the back row as well as in the front. Do not use low power at any time!

4. *Improve your diction*

   Enunciate! Develop full tones and resonance.

5. *Develop your own style—be yourself!*

   Stop imitating someone else's technique. It's all right to walk for a time in the shadow of someone you admire. But don't make this forever. Cast your own shadow so that others may follow YOU.

6. *Record your voice—then listen to it*

   As indicated earlier, a recording of your voice can be frightening and illuminating at the same time. Pick out your faults. Eliminate the defects. Make more recordings as you go and note the pleasurable change.

7. *Take vocal or speech training where possible*

Take advantage of the Dale Carnegie and similar courses that are given year after year in your neighborhood, department store, library, chamber of commerce, insurance company or industry.

8. *Determine the words per minute that makes your best delivery*

You may be at your best at 135 words per minute. Your delivery may exceed 150. Work it out! You may want to deliver words of impact only at the rate of 100 words per minute, as is done in an average radio commercial. Think too in terms of change of pace. Think of emotional impact and mood. Short, clipped sentences roll faster. Long sentences slow you down. They may also put an audience to sleep.

9. *Rehearse tough words and tongue-twisters*

Develop the habit of toying or playing with tongue-twister phrases. It is not only a stimulating pastime, but it raises your reading-alertness level. It familiarizes your tongue and provides "muscle memory" for the tongue and face muscles. The "how now brown cow" and the "big bad bear" routines are still good for more than laughs.

10. *Be thoroughly prepared to speak*

11. *Never apologize to an audience*

Even though it's your initial effort at public speaking, never apologize for amateur status. The mark of the amateur is obvious enough, so don't spotlight it. Just be sincere. Throw yourself into it. If they get the message loud and clear they will stop seeing or hearing your faults.

12. *Speak with confidence, competence, and lusty power*

No one can resist the attractiveness of a positive speaker. So make your message vibrant! Make it believable and understandable as well! Touch their tender zones with purpose. Prod them a little. Get through to them as you touch the right buttons and enter those seven magic doors of sensitivity.

13. *Create the "common bond" that welds others to you*

14. *Hit the subjects that are close to home*

There are certain things that never die. Call them yesterday's truisms if you like, but they are still as strong today as they were a thousand years ago. The subjects that are still attractive are: *human dignity, charity,* and *service to others.* These, and others of which you are well aware, are "old-fashioned" but still remain vital because they have a lasting truth that deals with the *wants of people.*

HOW TO INCREASE WORD POWER

*Don't be an
Alice in Blunderland:*

1. *Read*
   Read aloud. Read often. Act out the role of the passage you are following.

2. *Use your dictionary constantly*

3. *Avoid all clichés and bromides*

4. *Pronounce your phrases—enunciate—give words meaning*

5. *Ask others to correct you for faulty speech*

6. *Study the material of great speakers*
   Determine what makes them great. Then use what you learn.

7. *Eliminate sloppy diction*

8. *Never use words until you know what they mean*

9. *Avoid words with double meanings that are subject to misinterpretation*

10.   *Use words with which you are familiar and with which you feel comfortable*

How to approach your audience

When you are introduced at a public gathering move easily to the stage, rostrum or microphone. No rush. Be natural as if you'd been doing it all your life. Be casual and *stand on both feet*. Don't lean against anything. Be intense but not tense. Keep track of your audience and that to which they are responding. Be sensitive. Discard immediately any material which consistently lays an egg. Keep developing new material. Don't be patronizing. Never tell an audience that it is wrong about anything. Lincoln said: "Preach hope. Never preach despair." Give them this hope. Educate them. Inform them. Spur them to action, but whatever you are after in talking with people, approach your audience with care. Once you have them in the palm of your hand pound your message across!

Use the words they know

How do you get through to people time after time? Use simple words—little words—like *love, hope, food, health, life* and *help*. Make these words plain. It's all right to think like a professor but be able to translate your thoughts to the level of the people with whom you are conversing. Keep the message plain and simple and repeat it over and over again. Render people a service by speaking in the language they know.

How to activate people through words

To get people to move in the direction you would have them go you have to use the procedure called *directional control*. To keep people corralled in a given groove you have to activate them into an action that follows such a groove.

There are significant ways you can effectively phrase your terminology to achieve this. Here are some methods of choice. Use them on one person or a crowd, but USE them:

WORD ACTIVATING TECHNIQUES
TO SET PEOPLE INTO MOTION

1. *The "Yes" Technique*

Get them answering in the positive. Get them nodding acquiescence. Hit them with one question after another as you play upon their wants and needs. Bring forth the "yes" response. Then deliver the "hook." Sell all the way!

Example:

"Do you want protection for your children? Do you want to prevent your wife's being molested in the streets? Are we going to put a stop to this reign of terror by young hoodlums who are turning our neighborhoods into havens of fear? . . . . Then here's what we can do!"

2. *The "Assume-They-Will-Act" Technique*

In this technique you simply DON'T temporize. Take nothing for granted. Deliberately TELL them the rules. Create no "ifs" or "ands" or "buts" or "maybes." You say—"You will do it this way!" and that's it! It's the method most often used on children, or by the military. It is regimentation by command. You tell them and assume they are adult enough to respond.

3. *The "Everybody's Doing It" Bit*

This is a social pressure technique that spells out whether you are keeping up with the Joneses. You tell them that you want them to have the best just like their neighbors, that Dr. Smith down the street just put in a colored television like this one, or, he's taking his wife on world tour, and why don't you! You follow through by telling how they can do the same, that they can have all the advantages . . . at less cost!

4. *The "Crash Finale" Technique*

This approach to persuading people saves the one big clincher for the conclusion of a talk or sales pitch. In this method you build to a climax. You attract, hold attention, play on heart strings, and activate the listeners. Then you hit them with the big solution. This is how it can be done. This varies from the "Yes" technique in that although you have hit upon their wants and needs you haven't asked for a "yes" response.

5. *The "Slight Exaggeration Angle"*

To emphasize a point it is often necessary to over-emphasize. By dramatizing your point, and building it up imaginatively it comes more strongly in public focus. You overdress the facts a bit to make them appear just that little bit more sensational.

6. *The "Technique of Denial"*

This is the method where you indicate that something is untrue, or that it does not exist, even while waiting for the opposite to hit the news wires. It's a "cover" or delaying action while waiting for the real action to break. This is a technique effectively employed by statesmen and politicians.

7. *The "Hustler's Pitch"*

This is the "big sell." This technique is used where you press the buttons of pride, greed, or charity. You not only salve their wounds but you appease their desire for recognition, for security and even for power. You press hard and unremittingly to make the deal click.

8. *"Take-them-into-your-confidence" Technique*

By giving the other person the feeling that you are sharing some intimate details with him you create a special bond. He enters your life, your experiences, and participates in your future. In actuality this doesn't happen, but through words you get him to feel that this is true. Permit the other person to feel that he can enter your life if he desires.

With controlled persuasion you are now directing people into given channels with words. You are using techniques for the purpose of giving people, or even yourself, direction. You are using words with design.

15

Let Yourself Glow
In The Art Of
Public Speaking

To develop an exciting new
formula for living, let
yourself glow! Glow through
the tinsel and glitter of words
and TALK YOUR WAY UP
TO SUCCESS! Develop the
self-sell in Personality
Appeal! Generate personal
magnetism and do a selling
job day after day under the
aegis of speaking in public.

T here are two parts of speech: the sender and the receiver. One talks. The other listens. The bridge of words between the two is called *communication*. It is also called conversation and you walk this bridge whether you are getting to one person or many.

In getting through to large groups of people there are particular effective "tricks" you can use in talking your way to success. For example, in delivering a speech to a big audience magnetize their attention with the following procedures:

Technique For Speech-Making

There follows, in brief, a method of communicating with a large audience. You talk. They listen. You create a bridge between yourself and them. To put yourself "across" and make your message stick, here are some particularly pertinent suggestions to follow:

1. *Pick out particular faces that are receptive to your message*

   Look right into their eyes . . . not over them! Watch for reactions. Note whether those faces are mobile with your ideas. Note whether they are alive with the emotional flow of your words.

2. *Lean toward these people as you address them*

   Put your message on a person-to-person basis even as your body appears to go out to them.

3. *Maintain changes of pace*

   Use the diminuendo and crescendo of words to make music in men's souls. Voice control is vital, so speed it up, slow it down. Dramatize your point effectively.

4. *Gesticulate without being a "hambone"*

   Make your gestures free, easy and natural. Smile, frown, but never dead-pan an audience. Keep your face alive. Keep your body alive. Make every part of you talk!

5. *Be forceful, direct, and get through to them!*

6. *Use subject matter worth listening to*

   Give them something that answers their problems. Give them something they need and want, something they can use. Be enthusiastic about it! Show fire!

7. *Use body control*

   Make your body portray sincerity and dynamics. Be poised, erect, moving. Keep balanced with feet slightly apart. Bring your sternum up toward your chin. Pinch your buttocks in and glow!

8. *Watch closely for symptoms of audience boredom*

   Actions, as well as faces, are a barometer of audience attentiveness. When the faces are no longer concentrated on you, when they become blank, disinterested, wooden, inattentive, when people slump down in their chairs, whisper, scan programs or newspapers or fiddle with their wearing apparel, hair, or accessories, you know that their interest in you has gone home.

9. *KNOW your audience*

   Know the wants and desires of people. Feed these wants. Make your attitude and theirs the same.

10. *Talk their language*

    Picturize your points but put them in language they know. Make them "see" it!

11. *Give them a message they can use*

12. *Be animate and forceful all the way*

    Punch your points out precisely one by one!

How to punch across a point

To deliver an effective message, Homer Abegglen, professor of speech at Ohio's Miami University, used to say: "(1) *Picturize your point* if you would get through to people. (2) *Illustrate* your point with a "pie," area charts, cartoon drawings, movie film, slides, chalk talk or graphs. In full view of the audience point out the facts. (3) *Provide statistics* that plump up your point. (4) *Use supportive quotes* from outstanding or well-known people. (5) *Give a few case histories,* (6) *Create contrast* to show how different one thing is from another. (7) *Compare* and tie your ideas to things which the audience understands. Let them visualize what you have to say. Use words and pictures so that they can *see* what you are talking about. Do some word-painting."

Picturize:

1. "United we stand. Divided we fall."

2. "As long as the monkey is on his back the drug addict belongs to the living dead. He slips in and out of hell through chemistry foreign to his body and soul."

Contrast:

1. "Yesterday it was a cowpath. Today a four-lane freeway."

2. Once it took Mom and Dad 30 years to acquire what you can have immediately today through installment-plan buying."

3. "Yesterday a pauper–today a king. He struck it rich in uranium."

Comparison:

1. "Today's *Hippie* styles are not new. It's 1920 all over again. The dirty, the unwashed, the miniskirts. Young people protest and rebel and know not why; like sheep, they follow in the pattern of slothful living."

2. "Raising taxes for higher government spending is like a massive economic leech that is bleeding our citizenry dry. Finally people will rise up and cry out."

Motivate Your Audience

Make people *want* to hear what you have to say. Make them *want* to go forth and conquer. Set off the word-firecrackers that influence their behavior. Don't just entertain them. Move them to action instead!

What is it that people want most?

People want security. They want love and affection. They want status, power, prosperity and a good name. They want recognition. They want to live longer and more graciously.

Within those *wants* lie your motivators. Show them how to make money and they'll listen! Show them how to protect their property and/or their lives and they will respond to your appeal. Show them how to enjoy new pleasures and they're with you all the way. Good men and bad men, good leaders and bad leaders, have used this procedure. Christ used it. Hitler used it. So did Mohammed and Jesse James.

Of course it's all selfish. Of course you are using words to appeal to human urgencies and wants. Of course you may be appealing to ideals, but DO it! Play the emotional chords. Develop the melody of desire until the person WANTS to act. When this happens you will have begun to talk yourself up to success!

In other words, MOTIVATE PEOPLE! Let them benefit by what you put into words. Let them gain something from what you have to say!

Speak up!
Make every word count

Success has many façades. The face that people see comes in the technicolor of sight and sound. To the average person success is something made up of material things. Within the area of his comprehension and wants he sees success as being represented by lavish homes, big cars, luxury living. He sees success as status symbols, but there's something more. That something is what he feels and how he acts when he is stirred with words. If he is sufficiently stimulated he will act to gain the status symbols he wants. *What's more he will act if what you say arouses, goads, or excites him to help create YOUR success!*

To prod people into action you have to speak up! The moment you start using efficiently those guided missiles of communication called words you will find yourself possessed of a new capability, a dynamic new power. You will be instilling the heartbeat of your terminology and ideas into the thinking of others and making them come alive. As this facility with words grows you will bounce off failure and frustration to achieve what you desire. When this facility with words comes, you will KNOW it!

Turn your own lights
on to light the world

The moment you become conscious of your ability to influence other people with words a light will go on within you. You will glow with it! When this occurs fears will dissipate. Self-assurance will put your best foot forward with no qualms about getting that foot caught in the door of the future. You will suddenly become aware of the giant within. When you become aware of personal potentials this inner power becomes the beginning of external success. It is the beginning of the realization that you are more than you thought you were or ever would be.

Move in on your audience
with strong vocal action

You were born to love. You were born to know that there are spiritual as well as social laws that control you, that the laws of words can make or break you and your *inner* as well as *external* success depends on whether you speak up and make yourself remembered as well as heard. Material success depends on your being front-line-center with the magic power of vocalization as you make a stand. Everything you ever wanted is achievable only with words!

When I say "words" I don't just mean TALK. I mean graphic words, action-packed words that are staged and dispensed as oral dramatics. I'm talking about having directional control of words with a target in view as you move your audience with strong vocal action.

Put your quarry on target when you fire

Aim and hit the hearer with facts, ideas and quality of performance. Let voice and body portray your message. Think of yourself as being on stage at all times. Hear yourself. In your mind's eye see yourself as your hearers see and hear you. Then deliver!

When you talk to people in private or in public are you poised? Controlled? Is your face alive, expressive with what you say? Are you posturally in balance? Is your *million-dollar personality* turned on? Are you watching your listeners for reactions? Is what you are saying getting through? Is your *forward-thrust* compelling?

The vocal approach
to being more compelling

A scientist once reported that it is the lower part of the face, not the upper, that gives away human thought. This is especially true of the open mouth.

When it comes to facing an audience the basic problem in winning success as a speaker is not the fear of people but fear of one's own inadequacy and failure. It is the fear of criticism.

All of us are bound by fears, emotions, inhibitions. The objective is to get rid of them. To get rid of the fear of public speaking you have to get rid of the fears that hurt your *public approach*. You have to get experience under your belt to do it. You have to learn to engulf your audience with words. How? In brief what are the "tricks-of-the-trade" that can be used?

HERE'S HOW TO ENGULF AN AUDIENCE
AND HOLD IT

1. *KNOW what you have to say and SAY it!*
2. *Don't memorize and repeat colorless speeches*

Take it from the top with know-how and put yourself in the spotlight. Make what you have to say bright and alive!

3. *Deliver the big message that people WANT to hear*
   Grip them! Hold their attention by filling their needs.
4. *Pound across themes they already know*
5. *Touch their emotions*
6. *Touch their vanity*
7. *Touch their hopes and prayers*
8. *Touch their pride*
   Like de Maupassant once said: "Make them laugh. Make them cry."
9. *Touch the zones of charity and goodness within them.*

In "giving a talk" set people on fire with your ideas. Build them graphically! Picture them! Step by step weave people into your *Impression Circle* and into the tapestry of your talk. After you have punched across your point, sum it all up. Give them something to think about and something to do. Give them something to take away with them and then ask for action!

Put your message across and stop. DON'T SAY THANK YOU FOR THE CHANCE TO BE THERE. Make no apologies. Believe what you have to say and SAY IT and others will believe it. Once you get them believing your way, quit while you're still ahead!

How Do You Characterize Yourself As A Speaker?

Now that you are becoming more conscious of yourself, and of words, how do you characterize yourself as a speaker? What is your opinion of your abilities at conversation? Have you ever made a self-estimate? Have you ever listened to a vocal recording of yourself and then wished that you hadn't?

If you have a recording of your voice put the tape or platter back on the machine. Turn up the volume. Listen. After you have stopped wincing take the following VOCAL CHECK-OUT CHART and fill it in. Do it as impassionately as possible. Stand back from yourself and impersonally inventory your vocal characteristics.

VOCAL CHECK-OUT
CHART

Note: *How do you see yourself? How do you feel you APPEAR to people? Check the following that depicts you when speaking in public.*

Word	Yes	No	Word	Yes	No	Word	Yes	No
Aggressive	....	....	Expressive	....	....	Proud	....	....
Aristocratic	....	....	Effective	....	....	Pithy	....	....
Arrogant	....	....	Frank	....	....	Punchy	....	....
Audacious	....	....	Folksy	....	....	Power-packed	....	....
Authoritative	....	....	Fiery	....	....	Quaint	....	....
Affected	....	....	Funny	....	....	Querulous	....	....
At ease	....	....	Fluent	....	....	Quivery	....	....
Adept	....	....	Fantastic	....	....	Reckless	....	....
Brutal	....	....	Feverish	....	....	Raucous	....	....
Bubbly	....	....	Flat	....	....	Roguish	....	....
Breezy	....	....	Gay	....	....	Rugged	....	....
Bustling	....	....	Glowing	....	....	Spirited	....	....
Bold	....	....	Gutsy	....	....	Sultry	....	....
Boyish	....	....	Goofy	....	....	Salty	....	....
Boisterous	....	....	Glib	....	....	Sarcastic	....	....
Benign	....	....	Hearty	....	....	Sunny	....	....
Brisk	....	....	Headstrong	....	....	Sympathetic	....	....
Boring	....	....	Happy	....	....	Serene	....	....
Conscientious	....	....	Honest	....	....	Sweet	....	....
Caustic	....	....	Humorous	....	....	Sophisticated	....	....
Cute	....	....	Irrepressible	....	....	Stirring	....	....
Crisp	....	....	Informal	....	....	Stormy	....	....
Cheerful	....	....	Imperious	....	....	Sad	....	....
Cynical	....	....	Insipid	....	....	Sloppy	....	....
Cocky	....	....	Jaunty	....	....	Soulful	....	....
Courtly	....	....	Jolly	....	....	Stately	....	....
Cool	....	....	Joyous	....	....	Smooth	....	....
Childish	....	....	Jovial	....	....	Tender	....	....
Collegiate	....	....	Lazy	....	....	Tense	....	....
Confident	....	....	Loving	....	....	Temperamental	....	....
Cordial	....	....	Listless	....	....	Tired	....	....
Crackpot	....	....	Lusterless	....	....	Urgent	....	....
Dreamy	....	....	Mocking	....	....	Uninteresting	....	....
Dynamic	....	....	Mystical	....	....	Unsatisfactory	....	....
Dominating	....	....	Manly	....	....	Unhealthy	....	....
Demanding	....	....	Melodic	....	....	Understanding	....	....
Diffident	....	....	Naive	....	....	Vivacious	....	....
Deliberate	....	....	Nice	....	....	Vital	....	....
Dignified	....	....	Natural	....	....	Vehement	....	....
Distinctive	....	....	Noisy	....	....	Worldly	....	....
Earthy	....	....	Nothing	....	....	Wholesome	....	....
Exuberant	....	....	Pert	....	....	Whimsical	....	....
Ecstatic	....	....	Passionate	....	....	Youthful	....	....
Ethereal	....	....	Pleasant	....	....	Zestful	....	....
Eager	....	....	Pallid	....	....	Zealous	....	....
Elegant	....	....	Personality	....	....	Zingy	....	....
Earnest	....	....	Pliable	....	....	Zippy	....	....
Effervescent	....	....	Pace-changing	....	....	Zombi	....	....
Extraordinary	....	....						
Explosive	....	....						

Cut yourself up impartially and bleed as you take this amazing step to a new and better understanding of yourself. Then act accordingly as you talk your way to success.

Now take the words you have checked. Put them together at the back of this book in the form of a paragraph. Then erase the marks you made on the chart and give the chart to a friend. Have him evaluate you as HE sees and hears you. Make a comparison with what you have listed for yourself. From the two concepts will then emerge significant facts about how you appear and how you sound when you are delivering a "speech." Yes, it's a rough and unprofessional evaluation, but *it puts your finger on some very salient points!*

Remember! Your Voice Is NOT What It Sounds Like To YOU!

Your voice must carry the mark of distinction

To make your voice personable to others, no matter how many defects or social clinkers it may hold, the secret to getting through to people in public speaking is not just hitting their emotional or physical wants but to provide a voice with a mark of distinction which people will remember. It should be a vital part of your Impression Circle, that aura of graciousness and charm around you.

Think it over. Think of your telephone voice and of people with whom you speak. Some voices are immediately recognizable. Such voices have distinctive timbre or quality. You remember them because they are "different." If your voice has no distinctive factor about it *then develop a message that IS distinctive.* Use your voice as the carrier for it. Play your voice like a musical instrument. Tune it if necessary. Develop tonal qualities as well as ideas that stimulate the imagination. Develop the feel-of-authority through speech even as you portray compassion, sympathy, understanding, courtesy and respect.

As you develop this new self-awareness, ask yourself the following pertinent questions:

SELF-EVALUATING
DEPTH PROBE

- Have I developed a speaking style that is convincing, unaffected, natural?
- Does it appeal to others?
- Is my diction clear? Am I understood?
- Do my lines pack punch?
- Do I use persuasive changes of pace?
- Does what I have to say have meaning and movement?
- Am I truly interesting to hear?
- Are my arguments enticingly offered?
- Do I speak just long enough and then quit?
- Do I sprawl verbally?
- Do I discipline my delivery?
- Do I express vitality and aliveness?
- Am I hesitant, timid, uncertain?
- Do I speak with authority?
- Do people apparently like me?
- Do I hold their attention?
- Do I keep using fresh approaches?
- Am I persuasive?
- Does what I say depict the real me?
- Is my style unique?
- Do I explode into vocal action and sell, sell, sell?
- Have I learned to think on my feet when the pressure is on?

Words Are Wants

As the means of expression words are used for personal gain. They are strategic weapons designed to gain friendship, gain gold, gain understanding or support. Their purpose is to supply a need. The *want* may be for sympathy or it may be for love. The want may be so simple as to describe a beautiful sunset or a lovely lady.

At any conscious or subconscious level the wants are there and they are felt and understood only in the medium of the words that make such understanding possible.

Because all human beings are insecure, they have to tie to something. They have to create, or have created for them, a bridge of words to God whom they would worship, to books they would read, to people with whom they would communicate, to the person or persons they would love.

Words, therefore, are forces that feed back and forth between people. They are lines of communication without end. They are forces with a future. They are wants.

Most word-forces are controllable

Some word-forces are non-directional. Some are misinterpretable. Dr. Jesse Nirenberg, director of psychological services, Tradeways, Inc., says, "People don't always say what they mean, with the result that what is heard is often misunderstood."*

The forward-thrust of some word-forces create surprising end results. For this reason, if you would achieve what you want out of life, if you would gain an objective, you have to control words that generate power within you, as well as control words which generate power in others! You have to snap your word-resources to attention as you convert the fertile valley of today's wants into the lush areas of the future.

> Words just wait to be used! Like genies in a magic lamp they await your command, so USE them! Use words as powers to gain your wants and be completely aware at all times that their power is YOURS!

Let yourself shine as you use them! Simply talk your way to success, because there's no better way to glow!

---

* Leon Davis Eldot, *Getting and Holding Your Executive Position* (Englewood Cliffs, N.J.: Prentice-Hall, Inc., 1960), p. 85.